# PRAISE FOR *DELUSIONAL* AND SAMANTHA ZINK

It is rare in this business to find an honest yet heartening account of what it takes to succeed. Samantha knows firsthand that there's no straight line or one way to "make it," but she's here to share what she's learned from over a decade of hustling. May we all learn to have the courage of our so-called delusions.

**—Allie Turner**
*Elle* Canada

Samantha does what society refuses to do: remind women that they are far more capable than even they could ever imagine. *Delusional* gives us a vulnerable and authentic look into the life of Zink, who combines her intuition with the guts to get to where she's trying to go—a winning combination. She reminds us that although the path to success is filled with hardship, the ones that make it are the ones who never give up.

**—Meghan Rose**
*Glamour*

Samantha Zink began managing influencers way before it was the cool thing to do. This fun, witty account of how she got her start is not only entertaining to read but can become a playbook for anyone who aspires to take a leap of faith and start their own business.

**—Marta Biino**
*Business Insider*

# DELUSIONAL

# SAMANTHA ZINK

# DELUSIONAL

## Confessions from One Intern's Rise to CEO

Published by Advantage Books, Charleston, South Carolina.
An imprint of Advantage Media.

ADVANTAGE is a registered trademark, and the Advantage colophon is a trademark of Advantage Media Group, Inc.

Printed in the United States of America.

10  9  8  7  6  5  4  3  2  1

ISBN: 979-8-89188-002-3 (Paperback)
ISBN: 979-8-89188-187-7 (Hardcover)
ISBN: 979-8-89188-003-0 (eBook)

Library of Congress Control Number: 2024911422

Cover design by Matthew Morse.
Layout design by Ruthie Wood.

This publication is designed to provide accurate and authoritative information in regard to the subject matter covered. It is sold with the understanding that the publisher is not engaged in rendering legal, accounting, or other professional services. If legal advice or other expert assistance is required, the services of a competent professional person should be sought.

Advantage Books is an imprint of Advantage Media Group. Advantage Media helps  busy entrepreneurs, CEOs, and leaders write and publish a book to grow their business and become the authority in their field. Advantage authors comprise an exclusive community of industry professionals, idea-makers, and thought leaders. For more information go to **advantagemedia.com**.

*In loving memory of NYC's IT girl. Your content was my biggest motivation before we even met. I will continue to share your beautiful soul to help raise awareness of mental health, especially in the social media space. Big squeeze, always.*

*To the dreamers who know they are destined for more. Don't stop until you get there! I promise it'll be worth it. Be insanely Delusional.*

*And to my younger self ... Who would have thought it, huh?! There was a time when we struggled and no one thought this would be our story. But we did it! We did something amazing and became someone great. I will always strive to be better and do better for you. Sky's the limit, S.*

# CONTENTS

# INTRODUCTION

*I don't belong here.*

That's the first thought that pops into my head as I prepare to walk the red carpet at the American Music Awards (AMAs). Growing up in small-town upstate New York, I'd watched my favorite artists attend the AMAs and soaked up every detail through celebrity blogs and magazines: the fashion, the music, the scandals.

And here I am. *Is this seriously my life?!*

I've splurged on the dress, a burnt-orange gown that makes me feel like a human flame. I've spent hours in hair and makeup. And yes, I admit it: I've practiced my pose for the cameras.

As my high heel touches the red carpet, I pause. I take a deep breath. And, for a second, I remember what it took to get here. From the days spent hauling coffees as an intern to the late nights spent starting my own business, it all flashes through my mind in a heartbeat.

And that's when I realize: *I so* belong here.

So, I throw my shoulders back, lift my chin proudly, and prepare to show the world: this girl is on fire.

\*\*\*

I don't usually measure my life in milestones, but attending the AMAs was a milestone that even I couldn't deny. But the truth is, most of my days aren't *quite* that glamorous. Especially my workdays.

Like today.

I'm trying to concentrate on a work call. But it's hard to focus when my dog, Ryder, can be seen sitting in the background. I shift my laptop to point the camera away from Ryder, a small white *Sato*, a mixed-breed rescue dog from Puerto Rico, who is now intently focused on itching his butt—on my brand-new couch, naturally.

I don't believe in offices. Even before the pandemic, I ran my influencer management agency, Zink Talent, which I launched in 2018, remotely. I've closed deals while in London, hopped on calls from the beach in St. Barts, and signed contracts before dashing to an aperitivo in Italy. My team is also fully remote, distributed across the United States. Remote work has its perks but also its challenges—like when your dog decides to showcase his butt-scratching skills mid-Zoom meeting.

Thirty minutes later, I've made it through the call without Ryder totally embarrassing me, and I move on to tackling my correspondence. I woke up to about five hundred emails, text messages, and DMs this morning. That's pretty standard, since I'm in Los Angeles (LA) but work with people from New York City (NYC) to Europe. Many of the people I work with have already been up for hours. I tackle the most pressing messages first and then consider hopping in the shower. But first: coffee.

I grab Ryder, and we walk to a cute coffee shop a few blocks away from my home in LA (yes, it's actually possible to walk places here; I was skeptical when I first moved here from NYC, too, trust me). The barista knows me and starts making my regular order before I've even paid—a honey lavender latte that tastes so good I could cry. This place has super laid-back Cali vibes, and I love this little moment of calm in my busy morning. The day is only going to get crazier from here.

I run through my to-do list in my head: *I have multiple calls with influencers, brands, and my team on my calendar. There are another three hundred messages to go through. Oh, and I'm supposed to head to my podcast studio in West Hollywood to record an episode of my podcast today. And then there's Ryder's dermatology appointment—can't miss that. And then I'm supposed to grab lunch with a friend. And I'm hoping to squeeze in a SoulCycle class later. And I've still got to pack my suitcase for a work trip to New York...* I pause, the thoughts swirling through my brain, take a deep breath, and try to clear my head. The to-do list can wait—for a few minutes, anyway.

I sip my latte and take an appreciative whiff of the lavender scent, letting myself soak in a moment and just *enjoy* it. Of the luxuries I allow myself since my agency took off, this is one of the most meaningful. I try to romanticize my day where I can. Maybe you do it, too—taking that extra second to admire your latte art (and snap a picture for Instagram) or to appreciate the sunshine on your face (and grab some footage for TikTok). A lot of social media is about romanticizing life's little moments. What's so wrong with that?

So, I give myself an extra second to savor that honey lavender latte. Because taking the time to actually *sit* and sip my morning coffee is a luxury that I could only dream of when my career first began.

## Do It for the 'Gram

Before I was the CEO of Zink Talent, I worked in public relations (PR) in the fashion, lifestyle, and beauty sector in NYC with a celebrity clientele, handling large campaigns and collaborating with renowned brands and designers. But before I got to do all that? I was an unpaid intern getting other people's coffee.

There was no time in those days for cute lattes and dog walks. But that was OK, because I was determined to learn from the best of the best in NYC's cutthroat PR scene and make my own mark. I've always been a doer, not a dreamer. When I decide I want something, I go for it.

When I was thrown into the brutal world of Manhattan PR after college (think *The Devil Wears Prada* but meaner, if you can believe it), if I was asked to do something, I just *did* it. If I didn't know what I was doing or how to do what I'd been asked to do, I went for it anyway. Fake it 'til you make it, right? I trusted in my ability to figure things out as I went along. And that confidence got me places—eventually. But first: coffee.

I swear, this is why I'm so obsessed with romanticizing my fancy coffees to this day—I'm still lightly traumatized by the coffee hauls I used to have to do. My boss would be holding a ten-person meeting and give me a scrawled list of every person's coffee orders. Even the handover of the list was scary, because my boss was a no-nonsense woman who had been in the business for decades. She'd seen it all, and she wasn't impressed by a new intern, especially if said intern screwed up the coffee order.

It might sound silly now, but at the time—I was twenty-three and *so* eager to shine—those coffee orders had me shaking in my boots, literally. My hands would be trembling when I got the list, and I can't tell you how many times I spilled coffee on the street or had to go back because an order came out wrong.

Of course, I wasn't just fetching coffee. As an intern, I did it all. I'd put together hundreds of send-out bags for fashion shows; pull clothing for photo shoots; run designer clothing all over New York;

hand-deliver look books to *Vogue, Harper's Bazaar,* and *Elle.* (Read: bitch work.) Why pay a messenger service when you can just send the intern, right? I distinctly remember handling dresses that cost more than my *annual* rent. But I didn't care—at least, not at the beginning. I wanted to learn by doing.

That "just do it" attitude (not #sponcon, I swear) is something I carried on when I started Zink Talent. After an epiphany on the NYC subway, I decided, *I'm going to manage influencers.* And then I started pursuing that dream, literally on the same day. At the same time, I continued to rise through the ranks in the PR scene. When opportunities came, I seized them. Eventually, I'd go from an intern getting coffee to a full-time publicist managing my own roster of designers. Through it all, I started taking steps toward my goal, such as brainstorming a name, buying a domain, getting a logo made, and more (I'll get into the details later).

First lesson learned: do the things. Even the little things. Immerse yourself in the world at every step. Pick up what knowledge you can and make every connection possible. I trust in the power of manifestation, and I believe I've manifested some amazing things in my life, from partners to jobs. But manifesting alone isn't enough. Hard work is another critical component to success—hard work plus confidence.

# #Instincts #Intuition #Inspiration

Back when I was hauling coffees for PR mavens, fashion editors, and models, I never imagined I'd be where I am now. And where am I now? I've just finished Ryder's dermatology appointment and I'm at lunch in LA, *sitting next to Austin Butler.*

OK, no I'm not sitting with him, but I can still admire the guy from one table over. I'm with a friend, and we're desperately trying to play it cool while discreetly enjoying one of the fringe benefits of life in Hollywood—the occasional celeb sighting. This one doesn't disappoint: Austin looks even better in person than he does on the silver screen.

This is the kind of working lunch I dreamed about in my early days in PR. When I started, I was interning for free and selling Michael Kors bags on the side to make ends meet. I was living paycheck to paycheck. While I was surrounded by haute couture and pricy designer brands—Chanel, Dior, Gucci—I was barely scraping by. I would have never dreamed that I'd one day be having working lunches at the kinds of upscale LA restaurants frequented by movie stars. Back then, even the dream of being able to have a sit-down lunch, instead of cramming a bodega sandwich into my mouth between work errands, was unthinkable.

I take another discreet peek at Austin. It should be illegal to be this good-looking. *What is my life?! How did I get here?* I take a sip of the fancy bottled water on the table—again, the kind of luxury I wouldn't have let myself enjoy when I first started out—and think back. And really, it comes down to the three I's: instinct, intuition, and inspiration.

As I forged my path, I listened to the instincts of my gut, the intuition of my brain, and the inspiration in my heart. I was a PR baby at a critical time in the industry, when traditional media was losing clout and social media was starting to realize its power. As a newbie, I was able to recognize the shift well before some of my senior leaders wanted to accept it. As I graduated from grabbing coffee to managing clients of my own, I found my voice and used it, often ruffling feathers in the process.

I was pushing for agencies to tap into the power of social media and collaborate with influencers before it was the norm. I conceptualized and managed an influencer collab at New York Fashion Week (NYFW) when the high-end fashion industry was *just* starting to take influencers seriously. I was arguing for the relevance of social media to agency leaders who viewed socials as a fleeting trend. It got me in trouble more than once (yes, I'll spill the tea, including telling you about the time I got fired). But I kept at it because I believed in my instincts, intuition, and inspiration.

Trusting my gut is what led me to my very first client for Zink Talent. I was still working in PR, and I hadn't even formally established Zink Talent when I signed her. She'd recently left a larger agency and was looking for new representation. I'd been working with her on the brand side of things, and I'd just had this epiphany about starting my own agency. So, I took her to coffee and told her, "I'm starting my own thing. Let me manage you. You don't have to work with me exclusively. Just give me a shot. Let me show you what I can do."

She had one million followers at the time, and the odds of her going with a new agency with zero experience were slim. But she agreed, and I hustled hard for her. I had a great network thanks to my PR experience, and soon enough I was securing her $10K and $20K deals, getting her on influencer trips, and hooking her up with dream collabs. We started working together in 2017; I officially founded Zink Talent in 2018; and now, five years later, she still recommends me to other influencers who need management. That kind of word-of-mouth reference has been critical in growing the agency. And it all started because I trusted my instinct to pitch her, even though I had zero experience in influencer management at the time.

Second lesson learned: trust your gut, even when people are pushing back. The ideas with big pushback are sometimes the best ones. Stay confident and believe in your instincts, intuition, and inspiration. They are your most powerful resource.

# Get a Little Delulu

Zink Talent has reached heights I would have never imagined. I now work with well-known creators who have millions of followers, as well as mid-tier creators and micro-creators around the globe. Zink Talent has done campaigns with some of my favorite brands: Celine, Dior, YSL, Armani. We've also worked with A&F, an amazing nod to my high school dream of becoming a store manager. Talk about a full-circle moment! In the wake of the 2020 pandemic, the business grew beyond what I'd ever anticipated, and I started hiring. I've now got a team of people working across the United States, from the East to the West Coast.

When people learn I manage influencers, they often ask me, "What's the craziest thing you've ever seen at work?!" But I'm going to keep it one hundred with you: my job is *not* glamorous! I spend most of my time behind a computer screen. Those work lunches with celebrity sightings aren't the norm—especially since the pandemic. What was once a lunch meeting is now often a Zoom call.

I want to be real about the unglamorous nature of my business so that no one pursues this path and gets disappointed. My time in fashion PR in NYC was much crazier than what I do now. But Zink Talent's success has created so many opportunities for me and my team, along with perks I never thought I'd experience, like flying first class (not regularly, but sometimes I treat myself).

I know a lot of people say that kind of success comes from having a strong vision and hard work. While that's true, I think the real secret is to let yourself be *just* a little bit delusional. Once I decided I was going to manage influencers, I pursued that idea relentlessly. I had to be scrappy. I ended up quitting my full-time, paid position with a PR agency, because I was *so* sure I could make Zink Talent work (my mom was worried, to say the least). What can I say: the delulu is strong with this one.

That said, I wasn't starting with nothing. I took all my experience from my years in PR and brought that to this new business of influencer management. I owe my current success to the many years I put in with various PR agencies first; my time in PR helped me build competence, confidence, and connections. Without it, I wouldn't be where I am today. I didn't wake up at age twenty-seven in a pantsuit and became a business leader overnight. I had previous experience to draw on—and, thanks to that, I believed in myself and figured things out as I went.

And when I say I figured things out *as I went*, I mean it. I didn't even have a business plan drafted when I quit my PR job and focused my full attention on Zink Talent. Even without a plan, I never doubted myself. To be honest with you, I still avoid excessive planning for the business. I work hard and pursue opportunities, always trusting my instincts, intuition, and inspiration.

My day-to-day life reflects this approach, too. I don't have a strict routine I adhere to; I'm not one of those entrepreneurs who gets up at five o'clock in the morning to work out and meditate. I'm not into routines—I left the nine-to-five office life behind for a reason—but I do love rituals. I keep a three-six-nine journal; I say positive affirmations; I express gratitude; I go to SoulCycle. Those are all small rituals that help me maintain my confidence and focus.

Those rituals help me keep my cool, even on the most insane days: those days when Ryder just *won't* stop scratching, and I've got five-hundred-plus messages to reply to, and I'm desperately trying not to ogle Austin Butler, and I'm wondering how I'm going to fit in a workout and pack for my trip and catch up with my friends.

You probably know how hard it is to try to *do it all*. It can get overwhelming. That's why I savor those little rituals—such as getting my lavender honey latte when the mood strikes and taking that calming moment to enjoy it before the day gets really crazy. I sip my coffee and remind myself it's all going to be OK. Sometimes, when times are tough, it takes a sprinkle of delusion to believe that—that things will work out. But I trust in it. And so far, it has worked out.

Third lesson learned: delusion can be your bestie. Delusion with zero action behind it can get you stuck. But delusion backed by action and confidence? That kind of delulu might just be unstoppable. That's the kind of delulu that gets you past hurdles everyone thought would trip you up. It's the kind of delulu that propels you from intern to CEO. It's the kind of delulu that gets you onto the red carpet at the AMAs in a fiery dress—ready to light the place ablaze.

# #Inspo: What's Your Story Going to Look Like?

I'm hoping that my experiences as I built Zink Talent—both the wins and the losses—can help you chart your path to becoming a boss in your own life, whatever that may look like. Maybe you're already manifesting your future or maybe you've got no clue what you want to do, which is totally OK. I sure as hell didn't have a clue when I started.

Still, I managed to forge a path to success because of three core ideals:

- *Be a doer, not a dreamer.* Take action. Don't just sit on your butt and scroll social media all day. That is, unless you want to get into the social media space, in which case you *do* have to be obsessed—more on that to come. Still, knowing what's trending on socials is only *part* of the job!

- *Follow your instinct, intuition, and inspiration.* Trust yourself. This can be really hard, especially when people are questioning you. Tune out those voices and listen to your own inner voice, first and foremost. Who else knows you better than you, right?

- *Get a little delusional.* Don't be afraid to embrace the delulu, even if it feels uncomfortable at first. Just *try* it. Remember the #tubegirl trend of 2023? Some people said it was delusional, but others said it was confidence. And I think "delusion" often is just another word for confidence. If an idea seems too "crazy" or a dream seems too audacious, don't write it off. It might just be that delusional dream is the one that's made for you.

This is my story. But it's also about you. This book is for the upstarts and doers of the world, the ones who aren't afraid to ruffle some feathers. Maybe you're interested in a career in social media or maybe you're simply curious and want some industry tea (it's coming—piping hot). Whatever the case may be, I hope you keep one little question in the back of your mind as you read: What's *your* story going to look like? You're the one writing it. Treat it with care.

# CHAPTER 1

# Not Going Anywhere

Confession number one: I never planned to become a CEO. I didn't have big dreams of getting an MBA, sitting in board meetings, and sporting a power suit. I sort of became a CEO by accident. When I was younger, growing up in upstate New York, I had *very* different dreams.

When I was in high school and even into college, all I wanted was to be a manager at Abercrombie & Fitch. If you grew up in small-town America in the early 2000s, like I did, you probably spent some time at your local mall and know the chokehold that A&F, Hollister, Victoria's Secret, and similar brands had on us at the time. These brands were *it*.

I got my first job in high school working at A&F, and I dreamed of rising through the ranks there, because that was my happy place. My parents got divorced when I was about fourteen, and it really rocked my world at the time. Now that I'm older, I understand that some people can't stay together forever, and I appreciate that my parents put our family's happiness first, even if that meant splitting up. But, as a teenager, I just didn't get it. I felt like I was losing control of my life; I had this thought of, *Why couldn't they have asked me first?!*

As immature as it was, I acted out. I rebelled. I stopped caring about academics and quit athletics—two things that were super important to my parents. I figured, *Well, if you're going to screw me over, I'm going to screw you over, too!* Again: immature. I just sort of skated by, not caring about anything, until I got that job at A&F. I loved it and threw myself into it wholeheartedly.

I started finding myself again in my community of coworkers. I made new friends, many of them older college kids attending nearby State University of New York (SUNY) schools. I gained a new interest in fashion (for a fifteen-year-old girl in the early 2000s, A&F *was* fashion, OK?!).

Looking back, I can see that the job and the brand as a whole had a toxic element to them. They hired attractive young people and placed a premium on looks, which definitely got in your head. There was a lot of implicit pressure—even if it wasn't stated, it was clear to everyone that if you were "pretty enough" (with "pretty" defined on their conventional terms), you'd get picked to work at the front of the store. I was too naive to see the negative implications of that back then and just thrived in what I perceived as "special" attention.

But overall, after having disconnected from my home life, I found a lot of happiness at A&F. I wanted to work there the rest of my life. That was my dream. I couldn't have pictured the dream I'm living today, because influencer management wasn't even a thing yet. How wild is that?

I didn't have a vision beyond A&F. When my high school guidance counselor sat down with me to talk about my future, including what college I would go to and what I would study, I was clueless. Like I said, I've never been big on having a plan. I knew that A&F *was* my future. Did I really need to go to school for that? But my family had always placed a premium on academic achievement. And my guidance counselor pointed out that I could always study something fashion related. Fashion merchandising sounded promising (one step closer to my dreams of A&F management? Sign me up!). So, off I went.

## Follow Your Own Crooked Path (Not a Guy!)

Confession number two: I followed a guy to college. *Cringe.* Although it worked out fine—I ended up graduating from the college I followed him to—today, I would never base my future on a man. But at age eighteen, it seemed logical. Why *wouldn't* I follow my dreamy boyfriend to an upstate SUNY school? I wasn't going to get in anywhere "fancy" anyway, as my guidance counselor had already assured me. My grades in my last years of high school were not great, and I don't even remember if I took the SATs.

So, when my boyfriend at the time headed for a SUNY school, I followed him, only for us to break up in September of the first semester. My family, already unhappy about my decision to go to a SUNY school, wasn't thrilled. My grandfather had set up a fund for each of his grandchildren to pay for their college educations. In his head, that meant at a prestigious Ivy League, not a state school, but he supported me, nonetheless. That fund paid for all five years of college (yes, it took me an extra year to finish), a gift I am deeply grateful for.

My grandfather also had pretty strict ideas about what to study at school. He encouraged me to pursue "serious" fields—computer science or nursing. I had first planned to study fashion merchandising, but the school that I followed my boyfriend to (sigh) didn't offer it. So, I went for a degree in PR; I figured I could always do fashion PR. My family didn't know what to make of my choice. I remember my dad asking me, "What *is* public relations? What are we paying for?" and I'd tell him, "Dad, it's similar to marketing." He was just not about it. But I'd grown up watching *Laguna Beach* and *The Hills*, and if I wasn't going to be an A&F store manager, PR seemed like a fun fallback.

Plus, to be totally honest with you, PR was a pretty easy educational path to pursue—which meant I had plenty of time for fun. Now that I'd finally left my small town behind, I wanted to socialize and meet new people. I started partying, maybe more than I should have, making the most of Greek life and going to fraternity and sorority parties. Even after having lived in New York and LA, some of the craziest events of my life remain those college parties.

With all that partying, my grades weren't exactly a priority. It wasn't that I wasn't intelligent; I just didn't care. If I flunked a class, I'd just retake it. Looking back, I can definitely say I didn't apply myself. I used to be more hesitant to admit that. Now, I'd say my views on education have evolved. I've read a lot of books and listened to many podcasts from successful entrepreneurs, and many of them don't believe in formal education. As for me, I'm not sure being forced to sit in a classroom and learn algebra prepared me for being a CEO. I think my years working in the trenches of PR taught me a lot more. Plus, the connections I made during that time were invaluable in launching my influencer management business later.

I think it's up to each person to figure out what tools and knowledge they need to forge their own path forward. Just because your whole family went to college doesn't mean *you* have to go, if it doesn't make sense for your career path. Or, just because nobody in your family went to college doesn't mean you shouldn't go. The most important thing is to go after what excites you. It's so cheesy, but basically, it's about what gets you out of bed in the morning. Back in my high school days, it was my job at A&F. When I went to college, I thought I was going to study fashion merchandising so that I could achieve that dream of becoming an A&F manager—then I veered off course and studied PR instead. Suffice to say, it worked out for the best.

This is also the perfect example of why I think having a super strict plan can be risky: it can get you stuck on a track you don't necessarily want to be on. Yes, it's great to have an idea of what you want, but I think it's also important to be open to changing directions. Forget what's trending around you and follow your own path, even if it's not clear or straight ahead. All those twists and turns in your journey may just land you somewhere wonderful.

Ultimately, I'm glad I went to college. I do think that having a bachelor's degree may have helped me get my first jobs in PR. And I can still remember how proud my parents were at my graduation. My dad showed up with this huge armful of roses and he got teary-eyed, which was definitely noteworthy coming from a man who never cried. I think my family secretly worried I might never graduate college, so they were so happy when I made it. My dad has passed away since then, so I look back on that day really fondly now.

# Hungry for More

Confession number three: I believe in listening to epiphanies—those wild ideas that drop into your brain from the universe, unbidden and unexpectedly. I've had a few major epiphanies in my life, and they've never led me astray. I keep my ears open for epiphanies now, because I trust that those "aha moments" are the universe trying to tell me something important. My first big epiphany was, *I have to be in NYC.* I knew that if I was going to be in PR, that was the place to be. The opportunities upstate were for things I had zero interest in, such as manufacturing and technology. NYC was *screaming* my name.

Again, I didn't have some grand plan. I was just following what I was interested in. Like I said, I grew up watching *Laguna Beach* and *The Hills*, and that had sparked my first interest in PR. I also loved *Sex and the City* when I was in high school, and let's get real: Samantha Jones was the ultimate #GirlBoss of her era, happily single and managing her own thriving PR firm in Manhattan.

You might think that kind of pop culture inspiration is silly, but here's the thing: it's still inspo! I think that you can and should find inspiration wherever you can in life, even if it's a "silly" TV show. Pay attention to what excites you and follow your instincts in pursuing that path. If your role model is a serious politician, athlete, or writer—Hillary Clinton or Simone Biles or Maya Angelou—that's awesome. But your role model can also be a fictional TV character. Samantha Jones was mine.

I figured that if I wanted to follow in my fictional idol's footsteps, I needed to get to Manhattan. So, I started googling fashion PR entry-level positions and quickly realized I was going to have start with an internship to gain some experience. I figured that if I could land the internship and crush it, I might have a shot at getting a paying role.

My Google search led me to a company called Dream Careers. They had a global internship program that gave you the opportunity to intern with companies in major cities across the world, from Paris to NYC. They helped with everything from setting up the internship to providing accommodation; for a small-town girl who wasn't quite ready to tackle the big city alone, it was perfect. And they had fashion PR internships. As I was reading about everything they promised on their website, it was like fireworks were going off in my brain. *This is perfect!* It was a dream come true—albeit one you had to pay for.

Luckily, I still had some money left in the college fund my grandfather had set up for me, a benefit of going to a lower-cost state school. So, I paid up and applied.

The program set me up with some interviews, which were done on Skype (this was the pre-Zoom era). No big surprise: I landed an internship. I can't be sure, but I assume that an internship position was basically guaranteed, since students paid for the program. I doubt I got it based on my interview skills, which weren't great back then.

The ensuing experience was impactful in a lot of ways. Since the program was global, I met young people from all over the world. We got to stay in the New York University (NYU) dorms, so we were right in the middle of all the action. And we were taught the ways of the big bad city: they literally set us up with Whole Foods gift cards, so that we wouldn't starve, and taught us how to use the subway. Looking back, it's sort of funny how much handholding there was. But, remember, I was coming from a small town upstate—I swear, I would have cried trying to figure out the subway alone! We also got to do all kinds of fun activities when we weren't interning, from going to see a show on Broadway to attending a game at Yankee Stadium.

That summer changed me in a big way. I met amazing people. I got a little taste of New York. I had my first hands-on experience in PR. And, most impactfully, I was exposed to a whole different world and way of life, one I had only seen on TV or in the movies up until then. Since the internship program charged a fee and the internship itself was unpaid, a lot of the people participating seemed to have a lot of money. My roommates were wealthy, and they didn't hide it: I was suddenly surrounded by Chanel bags, Cartier bracelets, and couture clothing.

I hadn't really thought about designer fashion until then. I'd thought A&F was the pinnacle of couture! I was clueless about this world. Curious about what the girls around me were wearing, I started looking up price points, and my jaw dropped. It was like watching *Gossip Girl* for the first time but in real life. Imagine sharing a dorm with Serena van der Woodsen and Blair Waldorf, and you get the picture. The beautiful clothing, the glamorous European travels (in first class?!), the Michelin restaurants—hearing these girls talk about their lives was insane.

It was a bit of a culture shock, to be honest. But it was also one of the best shocks of my life because *it made me hungry*. I caught a glimpse of this lifestyle that had only existed in fictional worlds. Now, I saw that it could be real. I wanted *in*—and I wanted to earn it for myself. I remember when I was about thirteen, my mom was driving me home from school when she asked me the typical, "What do you want to be when you grow up?" question. I told her I wanted to marry rich—some remnant of the helpless princess waiting for her knight in shining armor that old-school Disney movies had impressed on me. She gave me a reality check *real* quick. She said, "Well, what happens if you get a divorce? Then you're left with nothing."

That stuck with me—maybe even more so because my parents actually did get a divorce. Ever since then, I've been determined to earn my own money. Some people would label me an alpha female, and I guess I am. It has brought its challenges when dating (more on that in chapter 9). But hey, if wanting to run my own company and earn my own money makes me an alpha female, then so be it. Ever since that fateful conversation with my mom in the car that day, I knew I *never* wanted to be dependent on a man. And when I got to NYC and saw exactly what money could buy, I was even more motivated.

I think having a vision is important if you're going to manifest the future you want for yourself. I think this is where getting a bit delusional can be helpful. I was twenty-three, with barely any experience, and I was dreaming of my future Birkin bag. Crazy, right?! Maybe it wasn't the most realistic vision, but it's the one that got me excited and taking action. A *little* bit of delulu never hurt anyone!

That hunger I was feeling got me motivated. And, again, I think that you should embrace whatever motivates you. It's similar to having a role model; it doesn't have to be all that serious, as long as it works for you. Figure out what makes you hungry. If that's exactly *nothing* right now, that's OK, too. It wasn't until my NYC internship experience that I first felt that gnawing hunger; before that, I was just sort of bopping around, trying things here and there. If you're feeling zero inspiration at the moment, my advice is to just keep your eyes open and be open to new experiences.

I hope this doesn't sound crazy superficial! I wasn't driven solely by dreams of Chanel handbags. And money was definitely *not* why I grinded in PR, because honestly, I didn't make much. Interns and junior publicists never do. I genuinely adored the work from the very beginning. I loved my internship experience and believed I had a knack for PR. It seemed like I'd finally, after some zigs and zags, found a clear path to follow. I now had some idea of what I wanted to attain in life.

Also, full disclosure: a lot has changed since then, and I admit, a new purse no longer sparks joy in the way it used to. That old cliché about money not buying happiness? It's kind of true. Without a *soul* purpose, money is just that. Money.

I believe in having a *soul* purpose in life, not a *sole* purpose—I'll share where I got this idea later in the book (a spiritual medium was involved—no joke). Finding your soul purpose means trying out different things. It means being open to changing course. It means not always sticking to your plan. Just keep exploring and, eventually, you're bound to find something that excites you.

Finding your soul purpose also requires believing in yourself. I've been a spiritual person for years—I like to think I was spiritual before it was trendy—and I believe in the power of acts like manifestation and affirmations. A lot of people I've encountered try to start a business or side hustle, and, even though they put the work in, they don't achieve success. In conversations with those people, I've often found that they don't really believe in themselves. They may say they do, but their mindset is actually holding them back.

I truly believe that you are not going to get to the place you want to be unless you genuinely believe you are worthy of it. If you're going to find your soul purpose, you need to believe you deserve it. I promise, it will make a difference.

# Empire State of Mind

Do you know that Jay-Z and Alicia Keys song, "Empire State of Mind"? It was playing everywhere in 2009; you couldn't escape it. If my life was a movie, that song would be the soundtrack to the part after I finished my Dream Careers summer internship. Just that song. On repeat. Once I got that hunger in my belly and decided that fashion PR was how I was going to get where I wanted to be, the lyrics of that song rang so true. To me, NYC definitely was the "concrete jungle where dreams are made of." So, when I moved home to upstate New York after the internship wrapped, I became determined to go back.

There was just one problem: money. Life in Manhattan isn't cheap. My Dream Careers internship hadn't led to the dream job I'd hoped for. But I didn't care. I told my parents, "I can't stay here. If you don't want to help me, that's fine, but I'm going back to the city." I felt stifled in my hometown. How could I go back to that life after everything I'd seen and done in the bright lights of the big city? It felt soul-crushing.

So, off I went. This was 2013. I scraped together the last bit of my savings and found a relatively affordable shared apartment on the Upper East Side. This was back in the days of Craigslist, and I found my roommate there. It was a six-floor walk-up (built-in cardio!), and I paid $1,200 a month ("cheap" by NYC standards). My room was so tiny; I had a lofted bed with a little ladder to get up to it and zero storage space. But I didn't care. I was back in NYC.

I started applying for gigs and landed a PR role soon after arriving—another unpaid internship. To make ends meet, I got a job doing sales at Michael Kors on Fifth Avenue. It was a high-traffic location, and the MK brand was booming at that time—every girl in America wanted the exact same MK bag and watch—so I hustled hard and made enough to get by, even though I was only able to work part-time, since I spent five days a week at the internship.

The internship didn't pay, but I didn't care. Yes, I was basically a glorified delivery person (this is the internship where I was fetching coffee, delivering look books, and carrying couture across town—all via subway, by the way, so those early lessons from the Dream Careers internship paid off). But I was *in it*. And simply being on the front lines gave me exposure and insights into the industry that I could never have gotten in a classroom. The major selling point of that internship was that it gave me the chance to get involved in NYFW, which is *the* event of the year for the city's fashion PR agencies. You haven't really done fashion PR in the city until you've survived your first fashion week.

So, even though I was barely scraping by, I was thriving. I started making friends through the internship and through my sales job at Michael Kors. Without realizing it, I was building a valuable network of connections that would help me to move up the ranks in PR and, later, to do my own thing. I did every random job I was asked to do, whether it was packing send-out bags or lint-rolling garments. And I did it *well*.

That was the other thing: the internship gave me a confidence boost. I had always been a self-assured person, but this role affirmed that PR was right for me—I loved it and I was good at it. As I proved myself to the higher-ups, I was given more substantial tasks. That's when I started getting more involved in the PR side of things. My bosses had me start pitching, organizing events, and working directly with designers. One of those designers would eventually help me move up from an internship to a paid, full-time position with the agency. I'll give you the tea on how it happened in the next chapter.

My final confession (for this chapter—there are many more to come in this book, trust me): half the time, I had zero clue what I was doing. PR can be very sink or swim. You're thrown into the deep end and expected to do things without anyone holding you by the hand. I didn't let that stop me. Don't let it stop you, either.

# #Inspo: What's Trending in *Your* World?

My path to fashion PR wasn't linear, to say the least. I really had no idea what I wanted to do until I did that Dream Careers internship after college. When I moved to NYC after that, I was convinced: *this is it*. I was sure that I'd found my calling and that I would be doing that for the rest of my life. Nope. Now, I'm in a completely different industry, one that didn't even exist when I was growing up. I'm not a manager at A&F; I'm not the Samantha Jones of NYC PR; I'm a CEO, running my own influencer talent agency. I've found my success because I'm open to the journey. Who knows what I'll be doing ten or twenty years from now?

I want to maintain that openness, so I try to keep these three things in mind:

- *Don't be so hard on yourself.* Show yourself some grace if your path seems to be zigzagging or you aren't sure what direction to go in. Just keep following the things that interest you. You'll figure it out.

- *Figure out what excites you.* If something piques your interest, take a closer look at it. Try out different things to see what gets your heart racing. Maybe you'll find out that something isn't for you after all. Or maybe you'll find something you love.

- *Get scrappy.* When you find something you want to pursue, get relentless. Work the side hustle to make ends meet. Sleep in the loft bed. Fetch the coffee. You don't have to have it all *right now* and, let's get real, odds are that you won't. I may have been dreaming of couture and first-class flights when I was twenty-three, but I also accepted that I wasn't going to have that overnight.

I definitely didn't have the perfect path. From not applying myself at school to following a guy to college, I took some steps that probably gave my parents sleepless nights. But it all worked out. I hope you can accept that your own journey probably won't be perfect. Above all else, don't worry about other people's opinions. What's trending in *your* world? Once you know, you can pursue it relentlessly. That's how you'll write your own success story.

# CHAPTER 2

## The Devil Wears Zink (Out)

"You went through my *personal* laptop?" I stared at my bosses—two women more than twice my age—my heart racing. "What the actual *fuck*?!"

I'd been working at my first PR-agency job for one year and had made my way from a baby intern to a full-fledged publicist with my own roster of clients. I'd been crushing it at work, but I'd also been feeling underappreciated (more on why to come). So, like anyone would, I'd started applying for other jobs.

On the day when I found the higher-ups going through my personal laptop (we weren't provided with work laptops, so we had to bring in our own devices), I'd called in sick. I think the bosses assumed I was skipping work for a job interview. Honestly? I was hungover.

It was one of the only times I've called in "sick" in my entire career. In the past, I'd always go in, even if I was disgustingly ill. I once even went into work with a broken foot! I am not condoning that kind of behavior, because I think health should always come first. But back then, it felt like I didn't have a choice—and I do think that willingness to basically bleed out for a job taught me how to hustle, which probably helped when I started my own business later. On that day, I was just so mentally done with that job, that when the hangover hit, I stayed in bed.

I was dating a club promoter at the time, and, I admit, I tended to get jealous when he was always talking to pretty girls for work. You don't realize how jealous you are as a human until you have a boyfriend whose job is to basically hit on the most beautiful women in the world. I was spending every night I could out on the town, in part because I loved to party—and *maybe* also because I was protective. It all added up to me getting caught up in the NYC nightlife, probably more than I should have. No, being hungover wasn't a great excuse to skip work—but it also didn't excuse my bosses going through my private laptop.

What they found confirmed their suspicions: I was applying to other jobs. At that time, the myth of no-questions-asked corporate loyalty was still strong. Discussions about what companies owe employees and topics like pay transparency weren't a thing. Companies weren't being held accountable like they are today; the expectation was still, "Take the pay you're given (even if it's less than you deserve), do the jobs we ask (even if those jobs aren't part of your job description), and don't question us (a.k.a., don't you dare look for opportunity elsewhere)." That mindset was even more firmly ingrained in my bosses, who were from an older generation.

When they saw that I'd applied to other jobs, they were done. They sent me an email, firing me immediately—with no explanation. Obviously, they didn't admit to what they'd found on my laptop, because it would have meant admitting to going through it. Meanwhile, I was at home, nursing my hangover with Gatorade and Advil, wondering what the hell had happened. Luckily, I had my spies in the office (my work besties) who messaged me separately to fill me in: *They took your laptop into their office—and it looks like they went through it?!* Well, that explained why I'd been fired.

There was just one problem: I still had to get my laptop back! It was my personal laptop. I couldn't afford to buy another one. So, I went to the office to get what was rightfully mine—and to give them a piece of my mind. I was ready to burn the place down. This girl was on fire, blazing with *rage*. This was my *personal* device. I had trusted my coworkers and my bosses, so much so that I didn't bother to put a password on my laptop (I know, not smart—trust me, lesson learned). How could they breach my trust by going through it?!

As I stormed back to the office, my anger mounted with every step. By the time I got there, I was ready to explode. And so, I did.

Right there in the open-plan office, in front of *everyone*, I had it out with my bosses. I was twenty-four at the time and still relatively new to PR. My bosses were industry veterans with decades of experience. A few years earlier, I might have meekly taken my laptop and apologized and gone back home. But in my short time in PR, I'd gained confidence, not only in my abilities but also in who I was becoming as a woman and what I deserved. And I deserved respect—more respect than I was being shown by two women who thought it was OK to go through my personal computer. I stormed out on the spot (said laptop in hand).

# Confessional: I Survived the Toxic PR Nightmare

*Chrissy, Samantha's former coworker*

I started in fashion PR when I was eighteen, doing an internship for a couture fashion house specializing in Italian luxury brands, such as Moschino. With names like that, we didn't have to chase the celebrities down—they came to us. Beyoncé would come by the showroom personally to put a shoe order in. I was a kid, so this kind of job was a dream. Eventually, that internship led to a paying job and started my accessories PR career. It was maybe $25K a year, which is pennies in New York, but still: it paid! And I kept at it from there.

It was about six years later, at another boutique agency, that I met Samantha. This agency was smaller and didn't have as many big-name brands—which made getting coverage harder. On top of that, we had a boss who came from the old-school editorial world and would promise clients things like *W* Magazine, when that was completely unrealistic. It was a struggle—but Samantha was a hustler. She showed up every day, dressed to the nines, with her hair and makeup done, and she *worked*. She did everything that was thrown at her. She was working the reception desk and then she also ended up having her own accounts, after one designer specifically requested her, because they saw that she was such a go-getter. She didn't complain, but I'm sure it was tough.

On top of that, the environment was toxic. I remember one colleague of ours who had curly hair was asked to straighten it. Another time, I was told I was "too ethnic" to appear at a certain brand's events.

Burnt out from the superficial fashion world and a cancer scare later, I booked a ticket to Bali, the farthest place possible from the Manhattan fashion scene. It was there I found my love of yoga, travel, and helping people physically, spiritually, and mentally. I realized quickly when I got home from Bali that I couldn't make a living just doing yoga, so I went back to school to become a physical therapist assistant. The field is extremely rewarding, and I get to do what I am passionate about—helping people. I still carry a Chanel every now and then (when I am not lugging a diaper bag full of snacks for my beautiful two-year-old, Bella), but it has a different meaning to me than back in my fashion days. My time in fashion wasn't all bad. I did meet some good eggs along the way, such as Samantha. I will never forget all my incredible experiences the fashion world brought me, as well as the bad and the life lessons it has taught me.

Samantha was still there when I left that agency, and I remember she wasn't happy anymore either. She was still doing the grunt work while also working on accounts; they were taking advantage of her. And then the whole thing with the laptop happened, and it was the last straw. If I remember correctly, they wouldn't even give back the laptop at first, which was nuts, because it was her *personal* laptop—how was she supposed to get a new job without it?! I can't imagine how scared she was, getting fired with no job lined up and having to survive financially in Manhattan. But sometimes when you're at a low point, it gives you the courage and strength to go out and do something big. And that's what she did.

The agency that Chrissy and I worked at together was probably one of the most intense. One of the women founders was adamant about not allowing chipped nail polish and would email the entire office about it if anyone came with it, framing it as a general "reminder" without naming names. This was before nonchip gel nails existed! Leaving was probably good for me. Still, it was scary.

When I stormed out of the office that day, I had no severance or another job lined up. Once the rage subsided, reality sank in. I knew I needed a new job—fast. What I didn't know? The best was yet to come.

# Give In to What Excites You (No Shame If That's Male Models)

Let's go back to the beginning. My exit from that first agency job may have been dramatic. But before it got to that point, that first PR gig was an amazing learning experience. And I'm still in touch with people from that office.

Pro tip number one: don't burn bridges. I don't cut professional ties, and it's helped me to build my business. When I later got my own company off the ground, I was able to call on many people for favors. It can be tempting to burn the whole freaking city down if you feel wronged or slighted, but that kind of vengeful rage doesn't do anyone any good, including yourself.

Having my first "official" PR job end in such a dramatic fashion sucked, don't get me wrong. But I learned a lot in that job. Every job I've had has taught me something. Often, I had to learn on the fly, without anyone to guide me. And that first official job in fashion PR is a prime example, because, with that agency, I went from interning to managing my own roster of clients.

A lot of people wonder how to take an internship and parlay it into a role. For me, it started with some swoon-worthy male models. Seriously.

While I was still an intern at that first PR agency, I was assigned to work the door at a press preview for a men's fashion designer whose work had been appearing in all the major menswear magazines and was generating a lot of buzz at NYFW. A press preview is different from a fashion show, as it usually takes place in an art gallery or similarly smaller venue. The models showcase the clothes, while media comes in and out to view the collection. For a menswear event like that, you might have press like *Complex*, *Esquire*, and *GQ* stopping by, as well as celebrity fashion stylists. A press preview is more intimate and (in my opinion) more fun than a fashion show. People can enjoy the fashion, mingle, and sip cocktails.

Of course, I wasn't doing any of that. I was working the door—just another day of intern bitchwork, spending all day with my clipboard, checking people in and out. I kept peeking behind me to scope out what was going in inside. I was intrigued by menswear at the time, because it felt more realistic and accessible than women's fashion to me. When I saw the insane couture dresses during NYFW, I just thought, *Who the fuck would* ever *wear that outside of a magazine shoot?!*

And then there were the male models. Look, I'm not trying to objectify these guys, but they were truly works of art, OK? It would be a crime *not* to look—like breezing by the Mona Lisa without a pause. (Confession: I later ended up dating one of them … he was one of Tyra Banks's golden boys, in case you watched *America's Next Top Model!*)

All that beauty in the room—fashion and male models alike—had me giddy. I was just excited to be there; even if I wasn't *in* the room, proximity to that kind of environment was intoxicating. Since I was working the door, I had to stay at the event all night. My coworkers from the PR agency flitted in and out, quickly making the rounds, sipping champagne, and bestowing air kisses on the people they wanted to connect with. Then they would jet off to the next event—while I was stuck at the door. I was used to the long days that NYFW demanded. It was the norm to work until ten o'clock at night and then go to the after-parties to network (and have some fun), and then do it all over again the next day, usually on five hours of sleep or less.

By the end of the night, when no new guests were arriving to check in, I was able to leave my post and explore the press preview. I was in *heaven*. Everyone was dressed so stylishly, the models were gorgeous, the new collection was amazing ... and then I started talking to the designer.

I remember being enthusiastic as he showed me the collection. I was that star-eyed emoji in the flesh, word-vomiting about how I liked this piece and that piece. I had no idea what I was talking about, but I was *excited* and gave my raw opinions. People who have been in the industry a long time tend to lose passion, so I think the designer valued that exuberance.

I didn't realize how *much* he valued it until a couple months later, when the agency I'd been working for that night held their holiday party. One of the agency partners came up to me and told me that same menswear designer had called him. Before he could go on, I was enthusiastically spouting off about how cool the designer was, how much I'd enjoyed meeting him, and how amazing his press preview had been. Finally, the partner got a word in edgewise, telling me: "The designer called me to say that he wants *you* working on his account."

I was *floored*. I had genuinely just wanted to share my love of the designer's work. I hadn't anticipated that it might lead to something like this. The senior partner went on: "I told him that you can't work on his account because you're only an intern."

Bummer. What a disappointment, right?

But then he continued: "So, it looks like you have a job with the agency."

*No fucking way.* That was my reaction. I'd dreamed of eventually landing a job after my internship, but I had *not* expected it to happen like that. A single phone call from a designer is what got me the role.

I remain immensely grateful for that opportunity—and I know it came about because of that unfiltered passion I showed for the designer's collection. In New York, a city of seemingly effortlessly cool people, I often felt out of place because of my natural exuberance. I was *excited* about everything (I mean, when I'd first come to the city for that Dream Careers internship a couple years prior, even taking the subway had been exciting)! My enthusiasm didn't match the "play it cool" NYC vibe—but sometimes, that paid off.

Pro tip number two: be loud about what excites you. Don't ever discount the power of your passion. Don't try to squash it down or mute it for other people. Let yourself get giddy and excited and enthusiastic. That's going to let you connect with the right people.

The holiday party where I learned I was going to become an agent was on a Friday. I started as a full-fledged publicist the following Monday. As the menswear designer's publicist, I did everything for him: sharing his collections with magazines, pitching him to media, and organizing interviews.

This was all new territory for me, because these duties weren't entrusted to interns. And there wasn't anyone there to show me the ropes. I was thrown into the deep end and expected to swim. It was a lot to figure out in a short time, and there wasn't any handholding. But that was OK for me. I've always been someone to go for it, and learning by doing was something I was used to.

Soon enough, that one menswear designer wasn't my only client. As an agent, I became responsible for a whole roster of designers, mostly in menswear, which became my niche. At the same time, the agency still expected me to handle my previous intern duties, from running errands (yes, I was still doing those dreaded coffee runs) to working the front desk. That meant checking in visitors, answering phones, and generally being a first point of contact when someone walked into the agency.

I had a lot on my plate, and I thrived in that buzzing busy energy. But I also found it weird that I was still having to do things like work the front desk. No other agent had to do that. I had five clients by that point, and I was always nervous one of them would come in while I was working the desk and ask, "Um, why is my publicist working as a receptionist?" It didn't feel professional.

Over time, I came to feel like the agency was using me, having me do the double duty of both an agent and an intern, and I started looking for other jobs—on my personal laptop, the same one that I used at the office (cue the ominous music). You already know how that turned out.

After I was fired, I still wanted to stay in PR; I was good at it and enjoyed it. Luckily, with the experience and connections I'd racked up (don't burn bridges!), it didn't take long to find something new after Laptopgate exploded in my face. The only problem? The next agency proved to be even crazier than the last. Thus began my wild and crazy ride through the world of New York's fashion and beauty PR agencies.

# A Spiritual Moment amid the Madness

I learned a lot during that first fashion PR job, not just on the job but outside of work as well. Because something happened during that time in my personal life that shook me to my core—and got me, unexpectedly, in touch with my spiritual side.

People are sometimes surprised to learn that I'm spiritual. In my younger years, I wasn't. But then something happened that made me believe the universe *definitely* works in weird ways I can't explain, beyond that there has to be some higher realm. Remember when I said I went to a spiritual medium? It's because I was trying to reach my ex-boyfriend in the beyond.

Let me explain.

This was a boyfriend of mine from my college days. We had been young and in love and partied together and studied together—it had been one of those wild, fresh romances with the kind of unhinged affection you can show more easily when you're younger and haven't been burned too many times before. He was a year younger than me, so he was still in college while I was already working in the city (which was part of the reason we'd broken up). Even though our relationship had ended, this was still a person I cared about.

And then I got the call. It was a workday, and I was at Starbucks (on a coffee run, what else). When a friend of mine from college called, I already had a weird feeling in my stomach, like my intuition was trying to warn me. My friend broke the news to me: my ex had died, unexpectedly and tragically young.

I must have been in shock, because it was like I was an autopilot. I finished the coffee run, returned to the office, and took my post at the front desk, sitting there with red eyes, sniffling away, until a senior agent said, "Oh, honey, go home!" I was so out of it that it hadn't even occurred to me to take the afternoon off, thinking it was better to sit there snot-nosed at the front desk. It wasn't exactly the first impression they wanted to give when clients came in!

A few days after that, I decided to go see a medium. I know. I had *never* been into anything like that before. The idea came like one of those epiphanies, whispering in my ear: *go see a medium*. Delusional as it seemed, I did. Maybe it was the grief. Maybe it was intuition. Maybe it was fate.

I did some research and booked a medium. When we met, I told her I wanted to connect with someone who had recently passed. I felt this deep need to speak with him. The medium cautioned me that she might not be able to reach him, given that his passing had been so recent. I didn't care; I wanted to try. I didn't give her any information about him, and there's no way she could have looked him up online or anything. She knew nothing about him.

But she still managed to connect me to him. She opened some kind of portal, and then she was talking as if she *was* him—he was speaking through her. None of it was vague. There were details about our relationship, our time together, intimate moments we'd shared—I remember thinking, *WTF*, because I hadn't expected it to actually *work*. But it was *him*. I was sure of it. So I spent the next hour talking to him through the medium.

One of the most poignant things that came out of that conversation was my ex's confession that he felt like he'd never had a soul purpose on earth. That broke my heart—and it was something I carried with me long after that meeting and have kept with me to this day.

Needless to say, that experience was transformative for me. I got very much into spirituality, which was a big deal, because I'd been raised in the Catholic church, where many spiritual things might be frowned on. I learned about psychics and manifestation and affirmations and laws of attraction. It led to a new, spiritually infused lifestyle for me, one that would carry over from my personal into my professional life.

I know a lot of this might sound strange to you if you aren't spiritual yourself. That's OK! I am *not* here to try to convince you of what happened or to force my spirituality on you. I'm just sharing my personal experience and how it changed me. I do think some of the lessons that I took away from my spiritual learnings might help others. Practices like meditation or positive affirmations can help anybody achieve greater calm and confidence, for example—on those points, there are even scientific data.

And I certainly think that having a soul purpose in life is important for all of us, whether we are spiritual, religious, agnostic, atheist—whatever! Knowing that you have some purpose on this earth can help keep you going through all the crazy shit that life will inevitably throw at you. At least, that's what I think.

# The Glitz and Grime of NYC PR

I've dealt with a *lot* of crazy stuff, but nothing was crazier than my days in NYC's fashion and beauty PR scene. From 2013 to 2018, I worked for five or six agencies in Manhattan, and they were all absolutely bonkers. No exceptions.

One of my bosses was literally famous in the tabloids for her aggressive outbursts. Gossip sites like *Jezebel* and *Page Six* featured horror stories about her constantly. She would yell all the time, and once she even came very close to hitting me—very Naomi Campbell of her! She was ruthless—but, as in every role, I learned a lot (including how to dodge a left hook).

Another agency I worked with was notorious for the mysterious meltdowns of one of its senior agents. He was this super classy, well-put-together man with a British accent. He was pretty closed-off about his personal life, so he was a bit of a question mark, which—with the accent—gave him a mysterious vibe. Overall, he was super straightlaced. But occasionally, he'd just disappear, without giving any warning. Inevitably, he'd return to his desk out of the blue, like nothing had happened, with no explanation. We never figured out why the agency's owners put up with his erratic behavior and assumed that he kept his job only because he was a personal friend of theirs.

At another agency I worked for, I was shocked to learn that one of the older publicists slept in the office. Not because he was staying late for work—we all had to pull an all-nighter now and then, especially in the runup to fashion week—but because he just didn't have a home to go to. In retrospect, I realize he was likely going through some turmoil in his personal life. At the time, as a twentysomething PR girl, I just thought it was weird.

Money was also an issue. As I climbed the ranks, I did earn more—but the salaries weren't great, especially for New York, where living expenses are high. One agency I worked for was consistently late in payments. I don't mean a few days late. They'd pay us four to six weeks late! I remember my mom trying to encourage me to take a stand and demand timely payments, and I just didn't have the confidence to do it back then. I'd tell her, "Mom, that's just the way it is, OK?!" In retrospect, I was taken advantage of more than once.

The world of NYC PR, at least as I experienced it at the time—maybe things have changed—is *brutal*. It took a toll on people, and they often coped in unhealthy ways. In one agency I worked for, it was an open secret that one of the partners had a serious drinking problem. He'd take breaks and come back *reeking* of booze. It became enough of a problem that he was muscled out by the other partners.

And those are just the day-to-day anecdotes. Things got even wilder during fashion week.

During NYFW, all the designers trust PR agencies to handle their shows. Running a show is a huge job. You have to check people in, get everyone in the right seat, and generally just make sure everything runs smoothly. Some people get into fashion PR thinking they'll have the treat of watching the shows—think again. Much of it is clinging to an iPad for dear life as you check people into the event (and you want to memorize all the names and faces of the guest list in advance—you *never* wanted to make an A-lister say, "Don't you know who I am?!").

I generally consider myself a confident person, but the pressure of NYFW got to me. My hands would be trembling when I was checking people into shows; I remember having a death grip on that iPad, afraid I was going to drop it because my palms were so sweaty. It felt like there was no room for error, and there wasn't. I know people who messed up at NYFW and lost their jobs as a result. And pretty much *everybody* I know in the industry has been reamed out by their boss at least once during fashion week. Consider it a rite of passage.

In general, PR agencies take on as many clients as possible because more clients mean more money. Now, throughout the year, various clients will have various campaigns at various times. But during NYFW, *every* single client in the fashion or beauty space will have *something* running—which means PR agencies are at maximum bandwidth. Of course, the big bosses who ink the contracts aren't the ones running around like chickens with their heads cut off—that would be me and the other agents, plus the freelancers the agency would bring on to keep everything under control, or at least to make it *look* like everything was under control. In reality, it was total chaos.

I'd be sprinting through hallways in my all-black outfit and high heels, trying to help with ten different shows at once. I and everybody around me were always *so* stressed out, because we knew that if a single thing went wrong, well, we might not get a cell phone thrown at us, but we'd definitely get quite an earful from the boss.

But here's the thing: I *loved* it. To me, it all felt glamorous and exciting. Maybe it was the lack of sleep making me delirious. I didn't care what I was doing, even if it was the most menial task, because I was *in* it. Whatever I was assigned to do, I was all in, whether it was placing name tags on chairs or fetching coffee for models (always the coffee runs! Are you starting to see why I'm now so obsessed with savoring my cute little honey lavender lattes in the mornings?!).

Now, working NYFW isn't just about managing the actual fashion shows on site in Bryant Park. A lot of the work happens behind the scenes. In the months leading up to fashion week, my coworkers and I would send out invites (yes, this was a time when paper invites were still a thing—I *never* want to lick another envelope again, please), handle RSVPs, create seating charts, and more.

There was also work to do after the show. That's when I'd have to sit down with a photographer to select photos from the runway show, approving which images to use. By this point it would be incredibly late, I would have been on my feet running around all day, and I was absolutely exhausted. But it had to be done.

Then, my job as the publicist was to get those images, along with a press release, to select online media—*Harper's Bazaar*, *Vogue*, *Elle*, and so on. We would target all the major websites, plus some of the more respected fashion blogs of the time (we would pitch to hardcover magazines a season or two prior; for NYFW, we would only pitch online publications). At the time, influencers didn't have the clout they do today, so that wasn't a common target audience—although I did have the opportunity to pitch influencers later in my PR career.

As a designer's publicist, my ultimate goal was to get them attention. The designers wanted people to be writing about their show—and, of course, they wanted to know *what* those people, the tastemakers of *Vogue* and the rest, were writing about their shows. So, my job was then to compile press clips and put together a press book to share with the designer. And designers aren't exactly patient about sighting their reviews—it's not a job that can be put off until after NYFW. I'd be compiling a press book for one designer between doing shows for other designers.

And then there were the parties. After long nights of manning the doors of various PR events, I wasn't about to miss out on a glamorous party! The underlings like myself would be the last to arrive, because we'd be stuck working late, while our bosses had already been sipping champagne and mingling for hours. But we didn't care, because we still got to go and that was all that mattered.

The parties were amazing, not only for the networking but also for the sightings. Grammy-winning musicians, Hollywood stars, supermodels, and more—all the glitterati seemed to congregate in New York for fashion week. I'd wrap up my workday, hit the fashion week party circuit, and then get up at six or seven the next morning to do it all over again. Oh, and I should add: I was going everywhere via subway. This girl didn't have money for an Uber or a taxi! (Plus, in New York, the subway usually *is* faster.)

By the time fashion week came to a close, I was exhausted. The devil wore Zink *out*. This girl needed a serious nap. But I was also exhilarated. You know that jittery, euphoric feeling you get when you haven't slept enough? It was like that, times ten. I was part of this awesome thing I'd read about when I was growing up in my small hometown upstate. *I was part of New York freaking Fashion Week.*

# The Last Agency

I made it through my time in the cutthroat PR world relatively unscathed. Of course, I was under-slept a lot of the time, because I was trying to *have it all.* The vibe in NYC was very "work hard, party hard" at the time. My PR friends and I would go out after work and show up to the office the next day totally hungover. I remember just staring at my computer screen, trying to look like I was concentrating when I was basically trying not to throw up.

The lifestyle I led back then is *not* one I would be able to handle physically or mentally (or would want) today. But back then, it was all part of the fun. I was young, fresh, and full of energy, so I thrived under the pressure. There's that saying that "pressure makes diamonds." I wouldn't exactly say I felt like a diamond—as much as I enjoyed the frenzied pace of PR, I was still overworked, and I recognized that a lot of my tasks were tedious. Maybe more like a Swarovski crystal. But that was OK—again, I was learning, making connections, and building the network that would eventually allow me to start my own company. Still, I had no clue that was where my path was headed. Like I confessed to you earlier, I *never* dreamed of becoming a CEO or owning a business. One thing that I *did* dream of was working with influencers.

When I wasn't hustling as a publicist, I was scrolling. Social media was taking off, and I was *obsessed.* I still am! I love to follow the fashion girlies and the beauty mavens, finding inspiration in the looks they create and the practical tips they give. I have a genuine appreciation for what they do, and I've never been shy about sharing that.

As I progressed in my PR career, influencers were gaining traction—and I was increasingly convinced that they were the future. Now, I should probably note that the "influencer" of that time was a little different from how we understand the term today. Influencers, especially in fashion and beauty, usually had blogs and used their Instagram (the medium of that moment) to push those blog posts. The Insta posts used grainy, preset filters and were less polished than what we see now.

And then there was the editing. People were even more intense with the editing at that time, and the tools weren't what they are now. I have photos of myself out with friends back then, where half of us have these squiggle, noodle-like arms, because we tried to edit the photos and didn't notice the weird wave effect it was creating in other parts of the photo. Even the "pro" influencers of the era would get busted with wavy doorframes and countertops behind them. I think a Kardashian even got caught with the suspiciously wavy doorframe once—and they're social media pioneers in the celebrity world!

It wasn't just the visuals that were different. The business side of the industry was different, too. In the very early days, influencers weren't getting paid; they were mostly working for freebies. And while the front rows of fashion shows are now often influencer dominated, back then, influencers were usually *persona non grata* at NYFW, especially the front row. Rumor had it that Anna Wintour even banned them in the early days.

Still, I was convinced that influencers were worth investing in, seeing them as being more accessible to everyday people, much like how I was drawn to menswear. And influencers seemed glamorous yet approachable at the same time, something that appealed to a lot of people I knew.

So, I pushed my bosses to work with influencers before many of them were ready to. My adamant championing of influencers as the future may have even gotten me fired on one occasion (don't worry, I'll spill the tea on *that* situation in chapter 6).

But I stuck to my guns and eventually it paid off. The last agency I worked for in my whirlwind NYC PR career was more open-minded than the others. They were going to let me handle all things social media and influencers. They wanted me so badly that they even offered me a signing bonus (no, it wasn't huge; yes, it still made me feel like a millionaire at the time).

This final agency I worked for could see that the media landscape was changing. Their clients were mostly in the beauty space, and many of them were already requesting to work with influencers. The agency wanted someone to focus on just that. By that time, I'd been in the PR industry for six years. I'd racked up experience at multiple agencies. And I'd been self-educating myself about social media and influencers, scrolling through my feed, reading influencer blogs, and scoping out interviews with some of the up-and-coming names. That "research" didn't feel like work. It was fun. A job that let me focus on influencers sounded like a dream come true.

I remember being so nervous going into the interview. I was still in my twenties, and the interviewer was this rich, powerful, PR boss who lived on the Upper East Side and had a chauffeured black car. She was likely in her sixties, but with rich New York women, you honestly can never tell. The TL;DR: I was intimidated. It felt like I was being interviewed by a real-life Samantha Jones. But I was determined to get that job.

My approach for the interview was to present myself as a hybrid expert, 50 percent PR pro and 50 percent social media maven. I highlighted all the experience I had from my previous agency work but also emphasized my social media knowledge. There I was, telling this sixty-something woman, "I *know* this stuff. I have the skillset. Let me teach you. Let me show you what I can bring to the table. I can get your agency more clients and help it move into the future."

In truth, I had *barely* worked with influencers at this point, just dabbling by inviting them to events here and there at previous agencies. My "expertise" came from simply being obsessed with social media, to be honest, but I *knew* I could do more. I guess it was one of those "fake it 'til you make it" moments.

But guess what? It worked.

Pro tip number three: sometimes you have to fake it. Just a little bit.

# #Inspo: What Are You Doing Today to Serve Your Tomorrow?

My borderline obsession with socials is what allowed me to present myself as a social media "expert" before that was even a thing. But hey, I *was* an expert—because I'd put in the time. Malcolm Gladwell suggests that it takes ten thousand hours of practice to become an expert in any given area. Trust: I've put in my 10K hours on socials, and then some.

When you find something that you love, throw yourself into it with abandon. You never know how your niche passion might serve your future career. Did 2015 Samantha think that scrolling social media for hours was going to ultimately lead to Future Samantha running her own company? Nope. But it did.

That said, it wasn't just getting low-key obsessed with social media that allowed me to succeed. These ideals helped me find my way:

- *Share your enthusiasm.* If you're passionate about something, advertise it. People are *so* jaded these days. A little enthusiasm is a breath of fresh air—and it can be contagious. When you tell other people what you're truly passionate about, you will start to find the ones who share your passion. And guess what, people *want* to work with others who are enthusiastic and engaged—case in point, my story with the menswear designer.

- *Invest in your education.* No, I don't mean get all the college degrees. You don't need a PhD. I mean *learn on the job*. I worked for many different agencies during my time in New York, and each one taught me something different (and valuable). From mastering the art of calming a raging diva to training my eye to know which fashion photos best showcase an outfit, many of the things I learned back then still serve me today.

- *Invest in people.* It's not just about what you learn—it's about who you get to know. Right now, you can't know how the experiences you're having or people you're meeting might serve you later. I didn't know it then, but my time in fashion PR was so important to later getting Zink Talent off the ground. Stay tuned, because I'll talk more about how I leveraged some of those valuable connections in chapter 4.

I had no clue where my career was headed, even as I started to work more heavily with influencers. But whatever I was doing at the time, I did it wholeheartedly. I let myself be enthusiastic about things that genuinely excited me. I learned at every step. I nurtured every connection. And when I faced a setback, like getting fired, I kept going.

My point is this: you don't have to have every detail of your life mapped out. It's such a cliché to say that you should focus on the journey, not the destination, but I do wholeheartedly believe that! We trumpet clichés for a reason, right?! They're usually true. So, if you're feeling a little bit lost in the world, that's totally cool. Just keep on giving it all you've got. Remember, you're writing your story as you go along. You never know what exciting places it's going to take you.

# CHAPTER 3

# Get a Little Delusional

"I'm going to start my own influencer talent agency."

The words just popped out of my mouth without me really thinking about them. It had been another long day at NYFW in the wild world of fashion PR, and I was riding the subway home with my coworker, Caity, after a long, sweaty, and hectic day.

"Oh my God, *do it!*" she exclaimed. She didn't even bat an eye. There we were, just a couple of delulu girls, rattling home on the noisy, smelly, chaotic subway—unknowingly planting the seed of my future.

Forget the fact that I had no idea how a talent agency was run.

Forget the fact that I had zero experience as a business owner.

Forget the fact that I was still at a super intense day job, working full-time in PR.

In that moment, none of that mattered. All that mattered was *the epiphany*. There was no premeditation or big thought going into my decision to start a talent agency. It was like the universe had whispered the idea in my ear and I, thankfully, decided to listen.

Ever since then, I've been careful to keep my eyes and ears open to what the universe may be telling me. Maybe that sounds sort of woo-woo to you—trust me, I get it. If you prefer, you can just call it listening to your intuition. When my gut instinct tells me something, I don't question it. I hope you'll do the same for yourself.

By this time, I was working at the agency that gave me the bonus to sign on with them and manage social media and influencers. In six years, I'd gone from a coffee-slinging intern to a full-time agent handling my own roster of designers. I'd survived one firing and more than one bonkers boss. I'd made it through twelve NYFWs (fashion week is held twice a year, in February and September). I'd gained experience and nurtured connections.

And, most exciting of all, I'd started working with influencers. In fact, on the day that I had my subway epiphany, I was on my way home from my very first legit fashion week event for influencers. Looking back, it was the highlight of my PR career.

Was it the biggest, most star-studded, glamorous event I ever helped organize? Nope. But it was an influencer event that *I* organized, from top to bottom—and it's the event that led to the subway epiphany. That's when I really came to appreciate the power of listening to your intuition; it can give you some valuable life guidance, if you'll let it.

# Look Out and Listen Up for Your Epiphany

This final agency I worked for in my PR career was focused more on the beauty space, not fashion. At the time, beauty was a little more welcoming to influencers. While the red velvet rope of the fashion world was still largely closed to social media mavens, beauty companies were realizing the clout they had.

In the past, beauty companies were major players in NYFW. They'd act as sponsors, because it gave them amazing publicity. Bobbi Brown, NARS, Maybelline New York—all the big players in beauty were there. These days, beauty brands are less focused on NYFW, instead prioritizing building direct relationships with consumers—for example, through social media. But at the time that I was in PR, NYFW was still a major event for most big beauty brands.

So, as you can imagine, I was thrilled when my agency announced we were working with CND, a nail polish company known for their bold designs and no-chip shellac. Learning that CND wanted to host an influencer event for fashion week excited me even more.

Once I got the assignment, I got to work right away. By now, PR felt easy to me. I was good at my job and comfortable with my tasks, so I had plenty of energy to get creative and throw my heart and soul into planning this event. But while I was a seasoned PR pro, I wasn't yet a pro at influencer events. I made some hilarious missteps as I put this event together that I still laugh about today.

I immediately started scouring social media for my favorite it-girls in the beauty space and created a roster of talent I wanted to work with. Then I put together a deck for the client to introduce them to the candidates. One problem I see now? They were all girls. Yes, I know, boys wear nail polish too! Things were a bit more "traditional" at the time; if I was planning this event now, I'd definitely have some guys in the mix—I mean, you know how much I like a male model, and let's face it, most influencers are basically models!

Once I had my pitch deck ready, I took it to the founder of CND. Meeting her was amazing; she was so quirky and crazy cool. I'd put so much effort into this pitch deck, picking my favorite photos from each influencer's account. After I rattled through my presentation, the founder said, "This is great. But I can't see any of their hands. I can't see their nails." She was so nice about it—but *yikes*, right?

It seems obvious, but this is something I still teach my new employees today. If you're going to pitch an influencer for a shoe collaboration, show their legs. If you're going to pitch an influencer for an earring collaboration, show their ears. If you're going to pitch an influencer for a hair collaboration, show their hair. You get it.

Despite that little flub, CND wanted to go ahead with the event. Basically, they wanted to invite influencers to NYFW to attend the shows that CND was sponsoring (which meant that the runway models in those shows would be wearing CND polish). They also wanted a pop-up where the influencers could get their nails done by a CND celebrity nail artist. The influencers could then showcase the brand's designs, which were sort of outrageous—we're not talking a basic French manicure.

CND gave me a budget—and then they gave me control. I invited some of my favorite beauty girlies, some of whom are pretty big today. I remember one of them had maybe two hundred thousand followers back then. Today, she's got over a million.

With the help of my colleague Caity, I managed the entire CND influencer event. From deciding who to invite to overseeing the actual pop-up tent, we did it all. And it was *so* much fun. I don't want to sound like a fangirl, but meeting some of the influencers whom I followed religiously on Instagram (the platform of choice at that time) was a dream. One of my biggest wins was working with @Bridget (1.3 million followers) whom I absolutely adored.

Meanwhile, the influencers themselves also loved the chance to attend NYFW and get their nails done by celebrity nail artists. Celeb artists can gain a lot of notoriety depending on whose tips they're tending to. Zola Ganzorigt (@nailsbyzola, 152K followers) is renowned for doing Hailey Bieber's nails, for example, while Kim Truong (@kimkimnails, 217K followers) takes credit for Kim Kardashian's nails.

The event was a success. The influencers were happy. CND was happy. And I was happy—happier than I'd been in a long time. At this point, having been in the industry for a while, I was skilled at my job; it was still a lot, but it felt manageable. It even felt easy. Too easy.

I was on the brink of getting bored and becoming jaded. That youthful enthusiasm that menswear designer had witnessed was in the past. That's an unfortunate fact of life that I stress about sometimes; when something is new, be it a job or a person, it's exciting and fresh. But as that once-new thing loses its luster, it isn't quite *as* exciting. It can still be comfortable and fulfilling, don't get me wrong. But that early-stage exuberance you once brought to the table? It's probably not going to be quite as strong.

I'm still super aware of this in my career now, which is why I constantly try to keep things fresh in life. At Zink Talent, I'm always trying to make the work new and interesting, looking for ways to innovate what we do. I don't want my team to get bored—I need them!—and I don't want to get bored, either. Because, to be honest, that's what happened to me in PR. The rat race became a merry-go-round.

By the time I was overseeing that CND influencer event, my love affair with PR was fading. Meanwhile, my love affair with the world of influencers was taking off. So, when the universe sent me that epiphany—*I'm going to start my own influencer talent agency*—my ears perked up.

Wild as it sounded at the time, I was receptive to the idea. That's what allowed me to then pursue it so relentlessly. I could have just shrugged it off, not said anything to Caity about it, and continued on my subway ride home. I could have stayed in PR forever. But I would have missed out on so much if I had.

The first thing your intuition will teach you, if you let it: dare to dream.

# The Social Network

By that later stage in my PR career, I wasn't just getting jaded with the work itself. I was also getting pretty fed up with the people. When I'd entered the field, I'd admired my bosses so much. I put the cruel and cutting Miranda Priestly types on a pedestal. They may have been mean, I thought, but look at what they had achieved! Being chauffeured to work in a black car, wearing the best designer clothes, sitting front row at fashion week—it was a dream that I aspired to myself, so I naively celebrated those who had achieved it. But after six years, the often toxic PR environment was taking its toll.

One issue with PR I had was the tendency to put client demands first, even if those demands weren't strategically sound or realistic. I would watch my bosses simply say *yes* to whatever the client wanted, even if it probably wasn't in the client's best interests. A client would say, "I want a feature in *Vogue*," and the boss would say, "You got it!" Very rarely would they say, "Well, print media isn't what it used to be. The landscape is changing. Maybe you want to go in a different direction."

Nope. They'd just say *yes*—and then leave it to the other people in the PR agency to deliver on whatever unrealistic promise they'd made to the client. Then, if something went wrong—say, the campaign in question didn't achieve the client's desired result—there was always a scapegoat to pin it on. And that scapegoat would be an underling, of course.

Even for small things, many of my PR bosses were quick to dismiss "the help," the lower agents, just to keep up appearances opposite clients. For example, if I didn't know someone I was checking in at an NYFW show and dared to ask for their ID ("Do you know who I am?!"), my boss would do damage control by dismissing me as "just an intern." Look, I get that client satisfaction is important, but feeling like your bosses *never* have your back gets old.

At the same time, I was starting to see the cracks in the veneer of the industry I'd aspired to conquer. PR was dying—at least, traditional PR as I'd learned it when I entered the business. Magazines were folding. Bloggers, not journalists, were in the front rows. And social media influencers were *the* thing among consumers. But a lot of people in the industry didn't want to see that, especially the more senior people who had built their careers on "the old way" of doing things.

Now, that's not to say *everyone* in PR thought that way. There were plenty of innovative, forward-thinking, open-minded people in the business who did see the landscape changing and who were trying to evolve with it. My final agency was a great example of this, embracing influencers while more traditional agencies were still shying away from them. As a result, that agency was a logical choice as the last stop in my PR career, allowing me to surround myself with supportive people who shared my vision.

By following my intuition and being vocal about what excited me—influencers!—I was eventually able to create a network of people who understood and supported my ideas. People like my coworker, Caity. When I told her I wanted to start a social media influencer talent agency, she didn't say, "What about your day job?" or "You're insane." She just said, "Do it!"

After my conversation with Caity, I immediately started taking steps to create my talent agency, setting it up while I was still working my full-time PR job. Literally the next day, I was brainstorming my future agency's name and thinking about everything from the logo to the website (I'll get into the nitty-gritty of those early start-up steps in the next chapter)!

Working full-time while trying to start a business was exhausting, and this is when my hard-partying days started to fade. As a NYC PR girl, I'd been fueled by the fear of missing out (FOMO) all through my twenties. I'm an extrovert by nature, and socializing was practically part of the job in PR. One agency I worked at would have wine and cheese at the end of the workday on Fridays, for example, and everyone would naturally drift off to explore the city's many bars, restaurants, and clubs afterward.

Now, I had a new focus. I didn't want to take away energy from my business with partying. I didn't want to be hungover. I wanted to have a clear head. My vision kept me going—as did my friends. They were super supportive of my side-hustle-in-the-making. But not everybody was.

My boyfriend at the time thought I was *nuts*. When I told him I was going to start my own business, the first thing he said was, "You don't even know how to budget." He'd always been harping on me to be more vigilant about my finances—in retrospect, he was weirdly controlling about it. We'd only been dating for a year when he started sending me budget sheets—and it's not like we were married and sharing money! In any case, he couldn't even *begin* to fathom the idea of me running my own business. His feedback boiled down to, "You can't even budget. How will you ever handle the accounting and all the other finances that go into running a business?"

The truth is, I wasn't even *thinking* about things like bookkeeping and tax filing at the time. The seed of my business idea had just been planted in my brain, and I wanted to water it and nurture it and help it grow. When you're at that stage, having someone, especially your romantic partner, immediately say, "There's no way you'll be able to do this," doesn't exactly help.

Well, guess what?

We broke up.

No, it wasn't (only) because he didn't support my business idea. There were plenty of other issues in the relationship well before my subway epiphany. But his lack of support for my business idea was a factor. I mean, if *anybody* is going to believe in your wild and crazy ideas, shouldn't it be your partner—the person who presumably wants to walk through life with you?

So, I cut the excess baggage and ditched the boyfriend. Instead, I surrounded myself with supportive people. At the same time, I started partying less and focusing more on my future. Instead of late nights out, I spent my evenings working on my future business. I journaled, meditated, and took my dog for long walks. I listened to podcasts about entrepreneurship and manifestation. And I fostered positive, healthy relationships with people who believed in me and my vision. I nurtured my network, trusting it to support me in the journey ahead.

The second thing your intuition will teach you, if you let it: who to surround yourself with. You know when you meet someone new, and you just get that *ick* feeling about them? You can't put your finger on it, but something about them makes the hair on the back of your neck stand up? That's a small nod from your intuition.

In the bigger picture, your intuition can help you attract the right people—the ones who make you feel *good*, who appreciate you, and who support you and all your zany dreams. Trust that instinct.

# All In(fluencer): From Side Hustle to CEO

The months after my subway epiphany were a blur. It was a tough balancing act, working full-time while getting Zink Talent off the ground—but it was working. I started making money. The only problem? That money wasn't matching my paycheck at the time, which was about $65,000. For that reason, I was hesitant to go all in. I wasn't ready to quit my job just yet.

And then I hit my breaking point.

The PR agency I was working for had overpromised and underdelivered to a client. The client wasn't happy, which meant that the boss wasn't happy, which meant that she was out to make sure the rest of us weren't happy. Remember how I said there always had to be a scapegoat when shit hit the fan? On that day, I was the scapegoat.

My boss screamed at me in front of the entire (open-plan) office. A room full of people watched silently while I tried not to cry. I remember that day *so* distinctly. My heart was in my stomach, and I was just so embarrassed. Even though I knew this wasn't my fault— the bosses had, as usual, given in to client demands and promised them something totally unrealistic—I felt like a kid who'd gotten caught doing something wrong. It wasn't unlike the feeling I had when I was fired.

I tried not to cry, feeling embarrassed and angry. I'd already started working on Zink Talent as a side hustle, but it wasn't making enough money yet to replace my full-time income. Still, the thought entered my head: *Should I just quit now?* Being a spiritual person, I asked the universe for a sign.

I'd thought for a time that PR was my soul purpose, but now, staring at my computer screen, trying not to cry, I seriously doubted it. I just kept thinking: *Universe, please. Just give me a sign, and I'll do it.* Nothing happened. So, I got more specific: *Show me 1-1-1, and I'll quit.* For those unfamiliar with angel numbers, a sequence of the number one means new beginnings, with the complete alignment suggesting you're headed in the right direction.

Well, no sign came, so I escaped for lunch. I went to Chopped for a Mexican Caesar salad to comfort myself. I was waiting in line to place my order when my phone buzzed; it was one of my coworkers checking on me. As I looked at the message, I saw the time: 1:11. The universe had come through for me. I didn't even wait to get my salad. I headed back to the office, cleared out my desk, and walked out. I didn't say anything to my boss, who was in a meeting. I just bolted.

You know those scenes in movies or TV shows, when somebody quits their job in some big, dramatic way and gives a metaphorical (or sometimes literal) middle finger to their nasty boss? Say, Bridget Jones storming out on Hugh Grant in *Bridget Jones's Diary* or Tom Cruise's character in *Jerry Maguire*. In the movies, they storm out to some empowering soundtrack with their heads held high.

My reality wasn't quite like that. The second I stepped out of the office, I panicked. I was newly single. I had insanely expensive NYC rent to pay. And while my side hustle was making money, it was still just that—a side hustle. I remember thinking to myself: This is nuts. *This is not a good idea. This is crazy.* For a split second, I even doubted the entire business and thought, *Maybe my ex was right. Maybe I can't do this.*

I was standing in front of the office building on the dirty sidewalk, trying to decide whether I should get on the subway and go home or slink back to my desk inside. Since I hadn't officially said anything to my boss, I could probably get away with it.

In a panic, I did what any twenty-something does in a moment of crisis: I called a friend. Lexi was a childhood friend of mine from upstate New York, and I'd known her for most of my life. She was living in Maine by then. I told her everything that had happened and asked her, "Do I get on the subway? Or do I go back inside?"

She didn't miss a beat. She was like, "Get on that subway. I believe in you. You need to do this." She even offered to loan me money if I couldn't make rent. I remember her being like, "I don't think that will happen, because I believe in you, but if you need it, I can spot you the cash." Again: *surround yourself with people who will support you*! I can't say this enough.

So, I did it. I remember riding the subway home in the middle of the day and feeling numb. In that moment, I didn't feel proud or confident, like some badass who'd just stuck it to their boss. My energy was drained. I got home and wrapped myself up in my comforter in bed like a mummy and just stayed there. I knew I needed to get my business off the ground, but I also knew: *today is* not *the day*.

I was a soulless body, totally exhausted. I just wanted to sleep. But before I crashed, I did do one thing: I emailed my boss. I told her that screaming at me like that was not OK and that I was leaving. And that was it. She never replied.

The next day, I woke up to a message from an intern I'd been mentoring at the PR agency, Kaleigh. She was part-time and not in the office every day, so she hadn't been there when I'd left; she'd only just gotten the news. I told her that I was going to start working full-time on my business.

That's when Kaleigh told me she wanted to keep working with *me*, even if I wasn't at the agency. She believed in my vision—just like Caity, Lexi, and so many other amazing people in my life. So, she ended up leaving the agency and working with me so that she could continue being mentored by me. In the early days, she'd come to my place, and we'd work in the lobby of my building because we didn't have an office.

And that was how it began—*really* began: me and Kaleigh, hunched over our laptops in the lobby of my apartment building. It was scary, as well as exhilarating, because I was convinced that my crazy subway epiphany was going to work. By that point, I'd already been working on my side hustle for about half a year. I had clients. I knew what I was doing. I wasn't earning a huge amount of money yet, but I trusted that, if I continued to put the work in, the money would come. And, in the end, it did—more than I could have ever imagined.

The third thing your intuition will teach you, if you let it: know when to go all in. At my core (and with a little help from my support network), I never doubted that I was going to be successful. That's what let me go all in.

Going all in also can mean knowing what to let go. This is my spiritual side talking: I definitely think you need to create space in your life for the good things to come, which can mean weeding out the bad things. I've lost jobs and thought it was the end of the world, only to have a better opportunity come along. I've gone through breakups and been devastated, only to realize he wasn't the guy for me. Now, when things don't work out, I know it's the universe telling me, "That was *not* for you!" So, I say, "Thank you," and keep it moving.

# #Inspo: Who Is Going to Support You on Your Journey?

If that screaming incident with my boss had happened six months before it did, I probably wouldn't have done anything. I would have let her scream, taken it, sat down, and gotten back to work. But by that time, I'd built the basis of Zink Talent and was ready to take it from a side hustle to a full-fledged business.

I want to be really clear about this, because the last thing I want to do is lead anyone astray: I did not blow up my life and quit my job to start a business from scratch overnight. Those superfast success stories you hear about on social media? I'm not saying they're all fake, but remember—social media is all about presenting yourself to the world a certain way. It can be pretty far removed from reality. I would know; it's my business!

Before I started Zink Talent, I spent six years in PR, gaining experience and connections. Before I dared to go full-time, I'd already started the business as a side hustle and had a small but growing client roster. Now, I'm definitely not saying you have to do it the way I did. Play by your own rules, not mine. Just consider this my official disclaimer: Samantha Zink is *not* telling you to completely blow up your life in pursuit of your dreams. Yes, I encourage you to heed whatever epiphany the universe may drop into your brain and to pursue what you're passionate about with wild abandon. But that doesn't mean you have to derail your life in the process.

Here's what I suggest instead:

- *Lay the groundwork for your vision.* You've had an epiphany— you know what you want to do with your life. You think you've discovered your soul purpose. That is *so* exciting! Now, what are you going to do to make that vision a reality? Give it some thought. It could mean formal education. It could mean hands-on learning as an intern. It could mean talking to someone in the business. Find your way in.

- *Surround yourself with people who support your vision.* Doing something like starting a business is scary enough; you don't need to deal with the weight of others' judgment dragging you down. Once you have your vision, share it. Blurt it out on the subway. Tell your bestie. Tell your mom. Share it with strangers on the internet. I don't care who you tell or how, but make sure you're building a supportive network.

- *Know your risk limit and pursue your vision accordingly.* Again, I don't want you to blow up your life in pursuit of whatever epiphany you may have. Doing something like quitting your job or starting a business does carry risk with it. Understand that and determine your appetite for risk, just like you would when investing money in the stock market. I had safeguards in place when I quit, like Lexi promising to help me cover my rent if needed. It wasn't necessary, but if it had been, the option would have been there. I wouldn't have gotten kicked out of my home. That's a big thing.

There are so many people out there who doubt themselves. When I decided to take Zink Talent full-time, I put all my chips on the table and bet on myself. And then I didn't have much choice *but* to succeed, because there were bills and rent to pay, and I had zero savings at the time. I don't suggest putting yourself in a super scary situation, where you risk something like losing your house. But I do suggest you *take action.* That's what separates successful people from non-successful people, in my experience. If you want to chase that epiphany of yours, you've got to be a doer, not a dreamer. Only *you* can write your success story.

# CHAPTER 4

# The Zink Way

"There's a taxi coming!" A New York yellow cab was barreling down the street toward me and my friends.

"Oh my God, perfect, let's get a bunch of the girls with the cab in the background of the picture! Girls, *go*! Pose, NOW!" My friend Jacob, camera in hand, scrambled to frame the shot, as my girlfriends posed in the middle of the street. It was ten o'clock on a Saturday morning in Manhattan, and I was with a small group of friends, taking photos of them for the newly born Zink Talent website—my baby.

Confession number one: The visuals on the very first Zink Talent website and social media pages weren't of influencers I was representing. They were my friends. I'd paid Jacob, who had a good camera, sixty dollars to take the pictures. Then, I'd called in favors with my girlfriends, promising them free coffee and a lifetime of gratitude if they let me take photos of them for Zink Talent's website and social media pages.

And here we were: a giggling cluster of twenty-somethings who had hauled their butts out of bed uncharacteristically early on the weekend after a night of partying, taking one more step toward making Zink Talent a reality.

"Careful, don't get hit!" I shrieked as the girls stepped into the road, eyeing the yellow cab dubiously. That car was coming *fast*.

Jacob was already crouched down, snapping pictures rapid-fire. "Got the shot!" he announced, jumping to his feet. "Now, get out of the road, you crazy bitches!"

The girls dispersed, screaming.

"Samantha, you *owe* us big for this!"

"Yeah, I can't believe I'm even up before noon on a Saturday."

"This talent agency of yours better make it big!"

I smiled and nodded, bursting with gratitude for these people, who were willing to help make my vision of Zink Talent a reality. Some of them were my close friends. Others were friends of friends or more distant acquaintances. All of them had agreed to take some time out of their Saturdays to support me. And yes, some of us were definitely hungover from partying the night before. But we rallied.

That was when I realized: if you put yourself out there, if you create something, people will have your back. Not everybody, obviously. But there will be enough people who are excited about your vision and want to be a part of it that you'll have the support you need.

Support like hauling ass through the streets of Manhattan on a Saturday morning, for no pay—just a few pictures. Those pictures were the basis of Zink Talent in the early days before I'd signed a single client.

Now, it looked like I had something real going on. A world of possibilities awaited.

# From A to Z: Building Zink Talent, Step by Step

When I organized the photo shoot to get images for Zink Talent's website and socials, the agency was still a side hustle. I was employed at what would be my final agency job while putting together the pieces of what would become Zink Talent on the evenings and weekends—whenever I could find the time.

Starting an influencer talent agency from scratch while also working a full-time job and not having a lot of money required me to get scrappy. Luckily, scrappiness is most definitely the Zink Way.

At that point, I knew nothing about running a business—and I made some (hilarious) mistakes along the way in the early days. However, I wasn't starting from scratch. Instead of focusing on what I lacked, I focused on what I *did* have: I had years of experience working for the top PR agencies in NYC.

I had an established network of friends, acquaintances, and professional connections, many of them eager to support my entrepreneurial endeavors. The photo shoot was only one instance where I called on my network for a favor, and it delivered.

And I had grit. NYC is a city of hustlers, and I'd learned how to hustle from the best of them. In PR, so much of my training had been hands-on learning, teaching myself while trying to keep up with the breakneck speed of a fast-paced industry. My time in PR had shaped me to be scrappy, innovative, and resilient. If there wasn't an obvious way to get something done, my bosses expected me to find a way regardless.

All of those skills and assets, tangible and intangible, helped me as I started building Zink Talent the Zink Way. I didn't have a lot of resources or money to invest. I couldn't hire people for everything.

So, I did a lot of the early business setup myself, and I figured it out as I went along.

But the most important thing was to just get started, and I didn't delay. I began working on Zink Talent on the same night I had my subway epiphany after a late night at NYFW. As soon as I got off the subway, I got to work. The first step: coming up with a name for my business.

## NAMING MY BABY

I took naming my business very seriously. I mean, how are you going to promote a business until you have a name for it, right? You're creating a name for your entire brand, a name that's going to be on your website, email, business cards, and socials. And that name has to last, because changing a business name later means lost recognition.

It was exciting; it really felt like I was naming my firstborn (which Zink Talent basically is). It was important to me to include my last name in some way, as a nod to my family. In retrospect, maybe I wanted to prove myself to them. With a family business on my dad's side called Zink Manufacturing, I wanted to do something similarly amazing with my own twist.

I toyed with the idea of Zinkism, like a religion, but thought it might be too vague. At the same time, I wanted to make sure the business name wasn't limiting. One of my dreams when I was younger was to work in music, for a record label or something similar (which is part of the reason that AMA invite was such a dream come true). I didn't take my business in that direction, but I still appreciate the flexibility of the name. And hey, never say never—maybe music is still ahead of me, one way or another!

I researched business names at my day job. I'd be at my desk in the office and have about ten browser tabs open, and half of them would be work-related content about NYFW, and the other half would be me googling things like "What makes a good business name?" Seriously. Like I said, I didn't know what I was doing when I started. I just started doing it anyway!

I settled on Zink Talent, which included my name, was clear, and was broad enough that I could work not only with influencers but also with musicians, artists, and creatives of all kinds. The options were endless; I didn't want to limit myself.

## THE BIRTH OF A BRAND

Once I had the name, I was able to take care of all those other admin components that go into building a brand. A lot of people assume branding is just about the *vibes*, but there are a lot of practical components that support a cohesive, well-established brand. I bought the domain name Zink-Talent.com; I created my email, Samantha@Zink-Talent.com. I still use that domain and email to this day.

The other thing I needed for my brand: the perfect logo. Now, a professionally designed logo can cost thousands of dollars. The really big brands will pay six figures for a logo in NYC. Clearly, I didn't have that kind of money. What did I have? Talented, creative friends. I asked a friend of mine who worked on the creative side of PR and had some graphic design experience if he'd design the logo for a small fee—I think I paid him less than one hundred dollars. Obviously, he did it for me more as a favor than for the money! And he did an amazing job.

It was a fast and easy process. I described my vision for Zink Talent to him, and I trusted him to get it done. He delivered three gorgeous options for me. All I had to do was pick one, and that was it. When it comes to working with creatives, this has been my go-to way of doing things, and it's worked beautifully so far. When I entrust someone with a creative task, I really *trust* them. We discuss my vision, and then I let them do their job, because I believe that I've chosen the right person for that job. The creatives I've worked with tend to thrive with that kind of freedom; that's when they deliver their best work. My friend aced the logo design, turning it around in two days, and that logo became the cornerstone of my brand.

Although the Zink Talent logo has been updated since then, I used that first design for years. I had it on the website, in my email signature, on my contracts—everywhere my brand was represented.

Of course, a logo alone wasn't enough for a visual brand identity, especially for an influencer talent agency. Social media is all about the visuals, right? When I made the Zink Talent website live, it was just a blank page with the logo and the words *Coming Soon* on it. That was it. I hadn't really thought this far ahead, so at this point, I stopped and realized, "Uh, I can't really approach people to represent them with a blank website!"

The only problem was that paying for professional models or photos was way out of my price range. Even buying stock photos was a stretch—plus, it seemed like if I was going to have pictures on my website, they should be my own. That's when I decided to organize that early-morning photo shoot with my friends in the streets of NYC. Those photos were the very first content to go on the Zink Talent website, and they were the cornerstone I needed to start approaching potential clients. Plus, there were all these other details I had never had to consider before in my professional career. There was a lot for me to learn, quickly and on the fly.

## THE BUSINESS SIDE OF THE BRAND

The branding side of starting Zink Talent came easily to me. I enjoyed the creativity that went into steps like developing a name or organizing a photo shoot. The business side of entrepreneurship? Well, that was a little bit trickier. One of the most common questions I get asked when people find out that I started my own business is, "Did you set up a limited liability company? A C-corporation? An S-corporation?"

For me, it was none of the above. I totally skipped this admin step. Because I could simply operate and file taxes as a sole proprietor, it wasn't legally necessary in my case, and so I didn't register Zink Talent as a formal business entity until I'd already been in business a few years. The most important thing to me was to simply *get the business going*. I wasn't stressing about whether I should start an LLC versus a C-corp or an S-corp. That just wasn't where my head was at.

I'm not saying that's the best way to go about it; I'm just telling you the honest truth about my journey (I told you I wouldn't hold back)! Figuring out business structures didn't seem as important as just *doing* it. Today, Zink Talent is a registered LLC. But that didn't happen for three years! That said, I do think it's worth talking to an attorney about your options if you're planning to start a business of your own. They can advise on what kind of structure makes sense for your business model.

Another thing I didn't do? Write a business plan. This was something that definitely stressed my mom out. She kept asking me about a business plan, and I just didn't see the point. I was more like, "Let me get this thing up and running and see what happens." I didn't want to bind myself to some strict plan; I wanted to just see what I could make happen. To this day, I *still* don't use a business plan. I'm worried it will limit me. Again, I'm not saying this is the "right" or "wrong" way to do business; I'm just sharing how my entrepreneurial journey unfolded.

# THE MONEY SIDE OF THE BRAND

Another reason I never felt pressed about creating a business plan was that I never sought investors (who usually want to view a business plan before they throw money at your company). I was still working full-time as I started building Zink Talent, so I had a steady income. But I was also living in infamously expensive NYC, so I didn't have a lot of money to put into my business. Some people asked if I was going to take out a loan or talk to investors. I never did.

I built Zink Talent for myself and by myself. In the early days, it was just me and interns doing the work. Later, as I was able to pay people, I started building my team. But I never asked for money from the outside. It was just me, believing in myself and taking some risks along the way. I felt more comfortable taking those risks if it was just my time, money, and energy at stake, not someone else's. There are some business models that require more cash to get off the ground, so investors or a bank loan are needed. But in my case, it wasn't a must. So, I skipped it.

One thing I *didn't* skip was getting an accountant. As much as I hated to admit it, my ex-boyfriend had been right about one thing: finances were not my thing. So, I hired an accountant early on to help me with the finances. It was a relief to know that my money matters were handled. What I didn't realize was that the first accountant I'd hired (someone I'd found on Google) wasn't great.

Confession number two: my first year of Zink Talent, I lost money. Part of the reason came down to hiring the wrong accountant. This is a mistake I hope you can learn from if you ever start your own business. The first accountant I hired for Zink Talent cost me a lot of money, in more ways than one. First, I had to pay their fee, which was I think $4,000 in that first year. Then, there was the money that I could have saved on my tax bill.

Here's the thing: I had no idea that it was possible to write off business expenses in that first year. Even though I wasn't putting a ton of money into the business, there were still expenses like registering my domain name, paying my friends for logos and photos, and setting up a work email. All of that could have been written off as a business expense, effectively lowering my business profits and, therefore, the taxes I'd have to pay the government.

I didn't know any of that, and the accounting firm I'd hired didn't tell me. They also didn't tell me that, as a business owner, I should have been filing my taxes quarterly, not just annually. Needless to say, by the time I filed my first official taxes for Zink Talent, my money was a mess. I paid way more in taxes than I should have and ended up with an overall loss that first year.

So I switched accountants, finding someone reliable through word of mouth. When it comes to the people you hire to support your business, I urge you to do your research. Don't assume that just because someone has the certification to be an accountant, they're the right one for you. My current accountant is amazing and has been with me for four years now. When you find good people, hang on to them!

## THE MENTAL SIDE OF BUSINESS OWNERSHIP

I've just talked about a lot of the logistical steps needed to start Zink Talent. Look, I know it's not the most exciting stuff—LLCs and accountants and domain names?! But I promised you I was going to keep it one hundred with you, and I'm standing by that promise. If you are going to start a business of your own, those "boring" parts are part of the package. And what's really cool is that, when you're taking care of those steps for your own business, they won't feel boring at all—because it's *your* baby. Everything, from picking a name to creating your website, will be interesting because it's meaningful to you. I promise.

If that isn't the case, then you might want to check in with yourself and make sure you *really* want to start a business, whatever it may be. Because one thing I've learned talking to a lot of different entrepreneurs is this: you will work hard, you will work long hours, and you will probably work even more than you ever did at a full-time job. But it probably won't *feel* like work. It's not the same as having a boss assign you a task that you *have* to do because someone else is making you do it. It's something you're doing for the passion of it. At least, it should be.

That mental component of starting a business is just as important as all the administrative logistics involved. In my case, there was no doubt that I was pursuing something I was genuinely passionate about. However, I still had to get my mind right in other ways. While I was taking care of all those practicalities, I was also doing a lot of internal work and educating myself about entrepreneurship. I read blogs by other entrepreneurs. I watched TED Talks on YouTube. And I listened to a *lot* of podcasts. Some of my favorites I had on repeat in 2017: *Almost 30, The Goal Digger, She Means Business, Him & Her, That's So Retrograde,* and *She Did It Her Way.*

I learned all I could from other business owners' experiences—the good, the bad, and the ugly. Hearing about other start-ups' struggles was both inspiring and educational. I'm hoping that my book can be that for someone else, which is why I'm talking about *all* of it—not just the crazy work stories and hilarious struggles and silly mistakes I made but also the business decisions I made. Because you deserve to hear it all.

# New Kid on the Block: How Zink Talent Landed Its First Clients

With the bare bones of Zink Talent in place, the next challenge arose: actually acquiring clients. Again, I did it the Zink Way, meaning I just went for it, without too much thought or planning. I used the resources I had at my disposal, the biggest one being the network I'd acquired through my PR career. And I took some risks in the process.

Confession number three: My last PR job was also how I landed my first clients. Basically, I started living a double life. The final PR agency I worked for allowed me to pursue influencer relationships. It was the perfect way to make contact with potential clients for Zink Talent, too. I'd set up brand deals and collaborations for influencers through the PR agency. When their contracts concluded, I'd take them out for a coffee, just the two of us. I'd sit them down, we'd catch up, and then I'd drop the bomb.

"By the way, I'm starting my own agency representing influencers." I think a lot of them were initially blindsided. At the time, "influencer management" wasn't really a thing, so none of these people had representation. I'd give them my spiel and lay out my business model: "I know you're not with an agency. Let *me* represent you. We don't have to be exclusive. I'll just bring you deals, and you take the money. I'll take a percentage of whatever deal I get you. Beyond that, you don't owe me a thing."

Now, I should point out that *today* Zink Talent works with influencers exclusively. That means that my influencers can't work with other agencies or brands directly. Everything has to be brokered through Zink Talent. But back then, I didn't have the credibility or experience to demand that kind of exclusivity. I may be a big dreamer, but I'm also realistic; I knew that, in my early days, I couldn't limit the influencers I wanted to work with. Today, it's another story. I've shown what I can do, I've built my brand, and I've got my credibility. Back then, I didn't have all that. I still had to convince people to work with me at all.

It was a good deal for the influencers, with zero risk—so most of the people I approached jumped on it. Because they'd already worked with me through the PR agency, they knew for a fact that I had connections and that I could pitch brands in a way that would actually result in real work (and real cash) for them. So, they mostly said yes. And why wouldn't they? They had nothing to lose. The risk—of time, effort, and money lost—was all on my side.

My double life was risky. I had to be careful not to let worlds overlap, which was hard when I was juggling two jobs. But the risk was worth the reward. I managed to get my first clients that way. As I started to build a roster, I gained the confidence to branch out further.

I started finding people on Instagram whom I wanted to represent and reaching out to them directly. This is where simply being straight-up obsessed with social media paid off. It wasn't hard for me to spend hours on Insta, pinpointing style, beauty, and fashion influencers whom I felt were inspiring (a.k.a., whom I was basically obsessed with). I figured that if *I* was obsessed with them, other people had to be too.

I'd send prospects a top-line email: "Hey, my name is Samantha Zink. I'm an influencer manager. I'd love to set up a call to see if we click and could work together." I'd also send them a list of some of my clients, simply providing their @ handles. When I first started reaching out like this, Zink Talent literally only had three clients. Of course, I didn't phrase it that way in the email! I wrote something like, "Here are some of the names I represent," as if there were more than that, when in reality, it was just those three.

Still, it worked. A lot of people would respond and agree to a call. Again, since I wasn't demanding exclusivity, most people were happy to hop on board. I was basically telling them, "You can do whatever you want. And I'm going to bring you deals." They could still take deals from other managers or agencies or brands. They weren't forced to go through me.

Now, when I *did* bring a client a deal, I made sure to draw up a contract. This is something I learned from my PR days: everything needs to be in writing. Everything. This is something else that I did the Zink Way. Did I hire an expensive attorney to draft my contracts? Nope. I looked up talent agency contracts on Google and found templates that I adapted for my own use. Later, I got DocuSign, which definitely made my contract management a lot easier. In those early days, I was just signing contracts by hand and scanning them. Was it the most streamlined, efficient, secure way to do things? Nope. Did it work anyway? Yup.

## Keeping a Business Going through Personal Crisis

The early days of Zink Talent were all about being scrappy. I was insanely busy, but I was happy pursuing a vision I truly believed in. Despite being totally overworked, I was having fun; my professional life was picking up. My personal life, however, was a bit messier, as I went through a breakup shortly after starting the business. We've all had to work through a heartache or two, so that's probably a feeling you can relate to.

But then I was faced with a much more earth-shattering event: the death of my father. My dad died on December 21, 2018, just as Zink Talent was getting more established. I was the eldest of kin, and because my dad didn't have a will, I was responsible for arranging his affairs. One minute it's a normal workday, and the next minute I'm on the phone with a medical examiner asking me what to do with my dad's body. I remember the medical examiner telling me I had twenty-four hours to decide if I wanted to cremate my dad or pay for a burial.

By default, I became the person to handle my dad's affairs. So much goes into the practicalities when someone dies; I was twenty-eight and had no clue what to expect. I was dealing with a family attorney, closing my dad's bank accounts, shutting off his electricity, canceling his subscriptions, writing his obituary—the list of things to do seemed endless.

At the same time, I was trying to keep Zink Talent going. I didn't have a choice—it was my only source of income. It was my own business, so I couldn't call in sick or really take time to grieve. This is one thing nobody really tells you about entrepreneurship: you can't step away, at least not in the beginning.

When I'd learned of my ex's passing years earlier, I'd gone to the office, sobbed, and been sent home to recover. The work of the PR agency had carried on without me, so I was able to take some time. When I learned of my dad's passing, that simply wasn't an option. Not if I wanted to make rent. Maybe Zink Talent also felt like a source of stability at the time—and, even if you aren't actually *relying* on your parents for anything tangible, when one of them passes, it creates an immense sense of emotional instability. At least, that's how I experienced it.

In any case, I worked through it. It taught me a lot. I compartmentalized. I bottled up emotions. I showed up. Having gone through that, I believe there is nothing that could throw me off my workday. A divorce. A breakup. A natural disaster. I think I could work through anything after having worked through my dad's death.

I am not saying that is healthy. I do think I have yet to fully mourn the loss of my dad. And I do think I could have let myself lean more on my support network at the time. I didn't even tell people back then, beyond a few friends, and I remember some of them being shocked when they found out after the fact. I'm not sure why I kept it so private, to be honest. And like I said, I'm not sure I've mourned that loss fully. Maybe that's something for Future Samantha to work through.

# #Inspo: What's Stopping You?

I made a lot of mistakes in the early days of Zink Talent. There's no doubt about that. But one thing that I got right was that I actually made moves. I didn't let a lack of time, money, or energy hold me back. As soon as I had that subway epiphany, I was like, "Great, let's do this. Let's go. *Right now.*" Over the years, the biggest mistake I've seen wannabe entrepreneurs make is that they wait. They're waiting for the right time, the right circumstances, and the right plan.

I believe there is never a "perfect" time to start a business. When I began, I had zero savings and was still working nine-to-five. That said, when I quit my job, I did have a safety net. Like I told you at the end of chapter 3, I had a friend who literally said, "I'll cover your rent," in case Zink Talent crashed and bombed. But part of the reason that friend made that promise to me was that I already had something going on. If I hadn't already started Zink Talent, I probably wouldn't have had the guts to walk out of that final PR agency job. Hell, I might still be working there today—or at another agency, feeling similarly unfulfilled.

If you take one thing away from this book, I hope it's simply this: don't hold back. Here are three tips to get you going:

- *Take action now.* A lot of people feel like they're held back by circumstances—not having budget or a team or time or not knowing what they're doing. Those things don't necessarily have to hold you back. When I started Zink Talent, I was a twenty-seven-year-old PR girl without a clue about how to run a business. I self-taught myself a lot. If I figured it out, anybody can.

- *Don't be afraid to ask for favors.* You may be surprised by who is willing to help you. I had so many people rally around me as I started Zink Talent, helping with photos, logos, and more. It wasn't just my inner circle, either. Some of the people in that photo shoot at the top of the chapter were mere acquaintances (one of them was Paige DeSorbo from *Summer House*, in case you're a fan—I didn't know her well, but she came out anyway). I think what I've learned is that if you are excited about your vision and what you're building, that transmits to other people. And if they're excited about what you're building too, and if they believe in it, they'll help you, more than you might realize.

- *Accept that you'll make mistakes.* Fear of mistakes can hold people back. Look, it's not going to be perfect. Accept that now. Accept that you will make mistakes and flail and falter and even fail. When I'm worried about things going wrong, I remind myself that if it doesn't work out, it probably wasn't meant for me, and that's OK. That mindset has helped me a lot. Don't let your limiting beliefs stand in the way of your success.

Now, if you're going to take action, you'll have to get scrappy. You'll have to put in the effort. If you're starting a side hustle while working full-time, like I was, you'll work late nights and weekends.

Yes, it might seem like a lot. But otherwise, you risk getting stuck and never achieving your dream. If you've got the grit—the resilience and determination to get up again and again when you fall down—you'll get there. There is nothing stopping you. I promise.

# CHAPTER 5

## Growing Pains

It was one of those amazing spring days in LA. Not too hot. Not too cold. Dry and rain-free, without a cloud in the sky. It was the spring of 2021, and the world was slowly creeping out of the pandemic funk it had been mired in for a year. And so was Zink Talent.

Zink Talent was holding its first in-person event. Since I'd founded the agency back in NYC in 2018, a lot had happened. I'd moved to the West Coast, Zink Talent had grown to levels I'd never anticipated, I had a team of interns supporting me, and we'd withstood a global pandemic and all the uncertainty and ups and downs that brought.

Now, it was time to celebrate. The Malibu mansion I'd rented for the event looked like something out of *Selling Sunset*. I'd hired an event planner and a sushi chef to set up a cute beach picnic. I'd flown out my interns, who were distributed across the country, for the occasion—a surreal moment. Just a couple years earlier, I'd been stressing about making rent. Now, I felt comfortable enough financially to rent this house and fly my team out.

We spent the whole weekend camped out in that Malibu mansion, celebrating. As it came to a close, I pulled aside Carly, one of my most trusted interns. Carly was actually the inspiration behind the whole event; she'd mentioned wanting to come to LA someday to visit me and meet in person. That's what sparked the idea for the event. Carly has been with Zink Talent since almost the beginning, since 2019, and meeting her in real life sparked another idea, too …

"Carly, you should come work for me full-time."

"Sure," she snorted. "I have a full-time job on the East Coast, Samantha!"

"How much are they paying you? I'm going to pay you more."

"You can't afford to pay me." She totally thought I was joking. To be fair, she'd gotten a look at my recent financials. She knew that my paying her would take a huge chunk of my profits.

Maybe it was the champagne. Maybe it was the fact that business had been keeping me up at night, worrying. Maybe it was just one of those moments of intuition, my gut telling me, *This is the right thing to do.* But I meant it.

"I'm definitely going to hire you one day. I don't know when, but I'm going to. Maybe in the next year or two."

At the time, Carly probably took my words as little more than empty drunken promises. But it wasn't long after that weekend that I called her. I asked her, seriously this time, what her current company paid her. Then I offered her more. We negotiated all the details of her contract, and she put in her two weeks' notice. There was just one thing left to discuss.

"Uh, Samantha, what's my actual *title* going to be?"

I paused. I was the founder and CEO of Zink Talent. Beyond that, the agency had a handful of interns. I googled C-suite titles.

"How about chief operating officer, COO?"

"Cool."

By August of that same year, Carly had joined Zink Talent as its first official hire and COO. Things would only go up from there.

# Confessional: I Was Samantha's First Official Employee

*Carly, Zink Talent*

When Samantha called me about joining Zink Talent full-time, my first reaction was to panic. Usually, we just text, so if she's calling me, I'm wondering, "Where's the fire?" I was immediately like, "Oh, God, what happened?!" And then she said, "I need you to quit your job and come on with me full-time. Like, yesterday." Obviously, I had a ton of questions, and I didn't quit my job on the spot. She gave me the time I needed to phase out of my other job. That conversation was in July 2021; by the end of August, I was working for Zink Talent full-time.

Those first few months were crazy. Samantha started Zink from scratch, so she was figuring out a lot as she went along. It was inspiring to see how hard she was working—but she was also barely keeping her head above water. I took over a lot of things that Samantha had been handling, like accounting. At the same time, I was working as an agent, pitching clients out, all while we were rapidly growing and still working with a team of interns only. Samantha had warned me, "The first few months are going to be a lot. I will need you to wear many hats," and they were. She was not joking. But we got things under control and found our dynamic as a team—and by December, we'd hired some full-time agents.

I had never been a COO before, so I was constantly learning on the job. I was twenty-four when I joined Zink Talent full-time, and I remember telling Samantha, "I'm going to be kicked off my parents' insurance in a couple of years. I don't need this right now, but I will eventually." She just said, "I totally get it. If you figure out how that works, we will make it happen." She had the same reaction when I asked if Zink Talent could offer a 401(k) plan; if I could figure out the how of things like company health insurance and 401(k)s, she was happy to implement them. But these are things nobody trains you how to do in college! So, I set up the calls with insurance companies and financial institutions and figured it all out. I had to be a self-learner, which is one way Samantha and I are alike, since she's always been a hands-on learner herself.

We've come a long way since those early days and are definitely more organized than we used to be. It doesn't feel like we're barely keeping our heads above water anymore. Being a part of that journey and seeing Zink Talent grow have been very rewarding. It all started with Samantha's willingness to do whatever it takes, and I love that I got to be there from almost the beginning to watch her rise.

Carly's joining Zink Talent as an actual employee, not an intern, was a landmark moment for me. When I first started the business, it had been a question of just paying my own rent. The idea of paying an employee had been out of the question. But as Zink Talent grew, the opportunity arose—and I took it.

# Pandemic Growing Pains: Seizing Unexpected Opportunities

When I started Zink Talent in 2018, I was barely making rent in NYC. By May 2021, I had moved my life to sunny LA full-time and hosted my first Zink Talent company event. By August 2021, Carly had joined as COO, becoming the company's first official non-intern hire.

Obviously, some shit went down between 2018 and 2021! Now, I promised you I'd give you the honest truth about how I got to where I am today. So, I'm going to lay it all out there right now: the COVID-19 pandemic was pivotal to Zink Talent's rise. It was growing pain number one for the company, with all the good and bad that can bring.

It's a weird thing to admit, because obviously the pandemic was this huge, traumatic, awful event that had terrible implications for people all over the globe. It was a time of massive uncertainty for everyone. For many business owners, it was also a hugely difficult time. Social distancing and similar public health measures forced entrepreneurs like restaurant and bar owners to close up shops or adapt their business models (e.g., to curbside pickup or delivery).

In the first weeks of the pandemic, like so many others, I was terrified. Zink Talent wasn't immune to the fear rocking the world, and the industry ground to a halt. Nobody was interested in social media collaborations and influencer promotions while the world was in such a precarious place. It felt *wrong* to post about things like skincare and fashion.

But then, with people cooped up at home, the online shopping boom began. Brands recognized the shift and saw opportunity in the moment. With everyone sheltering in place, companies were pivoting to push things like sweat sets. At-home athleisure became the new corporate uniform. Meanwhile, everyone was scrambling to DIY the things they'd previously left the house for; nail kits, spray tans, eyebrow tints, and haircare products were selling big. And a lot of that selling was being done via social media, with many people stuck at home with more time to scroll than ever before.

The early weeks of the COVID-19 pandemic were some of the scariest I've ever experienced as a business owner. Then, when business *really* picked up, they became scary for a different reason: we were scrambling to keep up as my team, our client roster, and our collaborations grew.

And I grew, too. There was a moment during the pandemic, when Zink Talent was taking off, that I felt myself itching to make a move. I spent the early days of the pandemic in Florida, with a guy I was dating at the time. I didn't love Florida, but I also didn't want to return to the dreary NYC weather and lockdowns. Although I'd only been there once before, LA seemed like a logical choice. The weather was good, it was still a big city, and it would be easy to connect to NYC for work when needed.

In the end, I made the move alone (well, not totally alone—my dog Ryder came with me), leaving NYC and all the memories it held of my younger self behind. My intuition definitely played a part; my spiritual side kicked in, and I felt like the universe was showing me the way. And I'm glad I listened to my instincts. In New York, I'd felt like I was always chasing happiness; in LA, I came into my happiness.

In a weird way, the pandemic was when I came into my own more fully, as both a woman and a business owner. Obviously, COVID-19 was terrible, with negative repercussions for so many people. I don't want to gloss over that. Some businesses, like mine, thrived; others closed altogether. As devasted as I was for those people and businesses, I have to admit that the pandemic was a turning point for

Zink Talent—though it brought us growing pains. If there's one thing the pandemic taught me, it was how to withstand turbulent times. It taught me that things can pick up after looking down. And it taught me how to scale up, *fast*.

By the end of 2020, I was making money I'd never seen before in my life. Remember how I told you about those early days in NYC, when I saw these other interns living the *Gossip Girl* lifestyle of designer handbags and red-bottom heels? Back then, seeing real people living the way my favorite TV show characters did sparked a hunger in me. It motivated me, kept me going while living in nasty apartments with roommates, hauling coffees, and dealing with *The Devil Wears Prada*–style bosses.

Now, for the first time in my life, I was able to live the lifestyle I'd aspired to all those years before. It felt like a dream, and honestly, it was an even better dream than I'd been able to imagine, because it had unfolded so unexpectedly.

Like I said, I'd never had a business plan or sketched out some step-by-step growth process for Zink Talent. While I'd always believed that I could do it, I never anticipated the level of success I did end up reaching. It was incredibly cool. I was able to afford my first apartment without roommates. I could eat at the restaurants I'd always eyed but deemed too pricey. I had the means to take myself on trips around the world.

It wasn't just about the money, though. Zink Talent's newfound success felt like some kind of confirmation, the validation that I'd done something right. When I set out on this path, I was sure I was onto something. And yes, my friends and family had supported my dream. But it had taken a while for the rest of the world to get on board. Finally, it was.

# Growing the Zink Talent Team: Investing in People

Even though Zink Talent was financially stable by 2021, hiring my first official employee wasn't something I took lightly. When Carly came onboard as COO, hiring someone meant cutting into the company's budget. Growing pain number two: learning how to let go of some of my money—and pay it to someone else! Honestly, part of me was afraid that hiring employees would mean giving up my newly comfortable lifestyle.

This is something I've found that people with successful businesses rarely talk about: once you start making money, it becomes *harder* to part with it. It's like, you've worked so hard to earn what you have, the thought of suddenly having a huge chunk of your earnings go into someone else's pocket becomes unfathomable. However, at some point, if you want to keep growing, it becomes necessary.

Learning how to invest in people was my second growing pain as CEO. Before I hired Carly, the company was running with just me and a handful of interns, most of them still in college, some of them recent graduates. At the very beginning, I'd only been able to offer interns hands-on experience. By now, I was paying them a regular salary, on top of incentives—for example, they'd earn a percentage commission on any deal they booked.

Now, don't get me wrong, my interns were *amazing*. After some hits and misses, I'd fine-tuned my vetting process and built up a team of people across the United States who understood the industry and had the dedication needed to get the work done. Some of the interns from those early days still work for me today.

The interns—or agents, as I called them—were mainly responsible for helping to manage clients. Each agent had their own pitch list. In the early stages, we didn't have an internal database or share contacts. As the team grew, I had to put organizational systems and processes in place, another growing pain that definitely taught me: get your shit organized from the start! It's way easier when you're starting from scratch.

When we started, we didn't even have a roster. We'd just send brands emails with links to our clients' profiles. Today, we put everything in Google Docs and keep a comprehensive database of our clients. We also use Beacons, which a lot of agencies use. It basically pulls your whole roster so that you can share it easily. And I still use DocuSign, the first piece of tech I ever invested in, for contracts. Tech like that makes life easier for me and my employees, who have always been hands-on.

Remembering my own days of doing bitch work as an intern, I knew I didn't want to give my team that kind of experience. No coffee runs. No meeting notes. No bullshit. I took the time to train my interns and teach them senior-level work, showing them how to make direct contact with clients and brands. I *trusted* them, which was something I'd missed during my PR days. As an intern, I'd often felt like people were waiting for me to inevitably fail rather than believing in me to succeed. I didn't want my own team to go through that experience.

The trust I put in my interns paid off. Some amazing people joined Zink Talent. I didn't care how old someone was or what their experience level was. What I cared about was that they were passionate about the industry and prepared to absorb what I could teach them.

Before Carly became my COO, she was one of the most amazing interns I had—and I found her through Facebook! A friend of mine in New York went to school in South Carolina, where Carly lived, and when I put a call out on Facebook looking for interns, that post found its way to Carly. She applied, I interviewed her, and we clicked.

Before I brought Carly on as COO, I did all the business admin myself. My interns helped manage clients, but that was it. Running Zink Talent required far more than simply managing clients. I was training my team and managing them. I was putting systems and organizational processes into place. I was coordinating bookkeeping and tax filing (with the help of an accountant). I was building the brand and promoting it. I was scouting new talent. It was a lot. All the while, Zink Talent's client roster was growing, and our collaborations were taking off. While the interns could help, they were only part-time workers. Most of them were still in school and that had to be their first priority, so I didn't have 100 percent of their time and dedication.

To be honest with you, I was drowning. I had so much on my plate, I literally couldn't sleep. I would be up at three in the morning, my brain going a mile a minute. Or, if I managed to fall asleep, I'd wake up in the middle of the night with some new thought: *What about that client? Is that new collaboration going OK? How is that new intern doing? Did I forget to take care of this?*

This still happens to me. When it does, I get the thought down in my phone's notes app and try to get some more sleep, sometimes shooting off an email. My team will be like, "Why were you awake at 3:00 a.m.?!" I'm very aware that Zink Talent's failure or success ultimately rests on my shoulders. I can't expect my employees to share that same level of responsibility. Some business owners might shove off their obligations to party in St. Tropez, but that's not the Zink Way.

Having Carly as a COO has helped. In retrospect, I may have waited longer than I should have to bring on a COO. But I wanted to wait until I was fully confident in Zink Talent's financial stability before hiring her. I mean, imagine if I'd jumped the gun and brought

Carly out before the agency was ready. What if I'd asked her to quit her job, uproot her life, and move to LA—and then had to let her go months later? I'm willing to take a lot of risks that might impact myself, but I don't want to take risks that could impact someone else's life.

Carly was my first official hire and the hardest, because I had to get over the mental barrier of "giving away" some of Zink Talent's earnings to an employee with a full-time salary. Still, it was exciting to make my first official hire—and more hires would follow.

A few months after Carly came on, one of my interns left for a competitor agency; they'd offered her a full-time job, which obviously paid more than her intern salary. It was completely understandable. However, it was also a wake-up call for me. I realized that my interns had zero faith that I might hire them once their training was done—because, up until that point, it wasn't something I did. Carly's hire had been the first. After that one intern left, I started regularly hiring out of my intern pool, selecting the most motivated to join the team as full-time agents.

I continue to hire from my intern pool to this day, and it's proven to be worth every penny, allowing me to grow (and to get some more sleep at night). You know those social media "gurus" who give investment advice? The only investment advice I'll ever give is this: invest in your team. That means investing money, effort, and time. In my case, it was a big investment timewise, because I was personally training every person from scratch. But it was time well spent.

# Growing as a #GirlBoss: Learning How to Manage

By the end of 2021, I'd started building a team beyond interns only. Zink Talent's client roster and collaboration deals were growing steadily. And I'd officially crossed over from solopreneur to #girlboss.

But I still had some growing pains ahead. Growing pain number three: learning *how* to manage people. Just because you have a team of people working for you doesn't mean you magically know how to guide them, inspire them, and keep them motivated.

I really didn't know what I was doing. One thing I did know: I didn't want to be like some of the nightmare bosses I'd encountered in my PR days in NYC. With Zink Talent, I wanted to do things differently. From operating fully remotely to avoiding traditional corporate hierarchies, I'll talk more about some of the ways I try to nurture a healthy, nontoxic work environment in chapter 8. For now, I want to talk about one of my biggest personal growing pains as a CEO—learning how to manage others.

Confession: leading others didn't come naturally, especially when it came to training them. Again, I wanted to do the opposite of what I'd experienced in my PR career, where there had been zero handholding; I'd been thrown into the deep end and expected to swim. I knew how terrifying that was. I didn't want to do that to my team.

I resolved to train every intern, every agent, who joined Zink Talent personally. I taught them from scratch, showing them how to approach brands, how to negotiate deals, how to draw up contracts—all of it.

Another confession: at the beginning, I wasn't that good at it. I would get impatient and, yes, snappy. I would get frustrated, feeling like I was taking time out of my day to educate someone else and wonder if my time could be better spent elsewhere. But deep down, I knew that investing the energy to train great agents would pay off in the big picture.

I would have these moments where I could feel myself channeling that *are you fucking kidding me?!* energy of my former PR bosses—impatient and angry. I didn't want that! I'd remind myself to pause, step back, and tell myself, "Samantha, this is *not* you!" I was taking these old ways of handling situations from my old bosses, and that was so against who I was and what I wanted to be as a boss myself. I wanted to do things differently. So, I did.

Patience was one of the biggest traits I learned as a manager. Yes, you can learn it; don't let people feed you bullshit like they're "naturally impatient." I had to accept that people would make mistakes. I mean, of *course* they would! I'd made plenty myself. Why shouldn't *they*? With the right training, the mistakes became fewer. And eventually, I'd get to see the people I'd trained become these amazing agents, crushing their goals constantly, and I'd get this sense of *pride*.

The more people I trained, the easier it got, because I started to see the rewards of effectively teaching my team. And today, I have an *amazing* team. I am so proud of my agents and what they accomplish, and I try to make a point to celebrate their achievements (again, something that never happened in my PR days). I'm constantly trying to build the team up, even for the small things—like, even a well-written email deserves a shout-out. I'm really determined to recognize the positives, because I think a lot of bosses only recognize the negatives. I want to celebrate the wins and hype up my people (I'll also talk more about the fun ways I reward my employees, from trips to lavish dinners, in chapter 8).

Why am I so keen on rewards? Well, for one thing, they're deserved. And then there's this (confession!): one of my biggest fears is a great employee leaving. I have CEO abandonment issues! Because once you've invested time and energy and money into training someone, once they're integrated into your team, the last thing you want is for them to move on. I remember my own PR days and how apathetic I was about the work toward the end of my PR career. I don't want that for my employees.

That's why I'm constantly trying to find ways to keep the work fresh and interesting and to give people opportunities for growth. I don't want them to leave because they feel like they're stagnating. I mean, growing pains can be uncomfortable for all of us, right? But feeling like you're *stuck*? That's even worse. I don't want it for myself, and I don't want it for my team either. I'm sure there are many more growing pains ahead. And all I can say is: bring it on.

# #Inspo: Are You Ready for Some Growing Pains?

I've had plenty of growing pains, good and bad, for both myself and Zink Talent. It hasn't always been easy, but, in the process of all that growth, I've built something that truly fulfills me. That has required persevering through the ups and the downs. It has required learning to trust others with my agency's operations. And it has required, above all, working on myself.

It's an ongoing process. In the beginning, I had to learn the business basics I described in chapter 4, from accounting to website creation. Later, I had to learn how to manage other people. Now, I'm always looking for ways to improve processes, get more organized, and create a more cohesive team. I can only do all that by focusing on myself—not comparing myself to others.

When I started Zink Talent, I didn't look to other agencies for inspiration. I had an idea and I pursued it relentlessly. I think focusing on my own journey allowed me to avoid the treacheries of imposter syndrome. I've never struggled to feel like I "belong" in my industry. Maybe part of that is because influencer management is still something that's relatively new to the world, even today. However, I think part of it also comes down to simply focusing on what I'm doing, not what others are doing.

Through all of these growing pains, I've learned a few things:

- *Know when to let money go.* Earning money is amazing. Letting money go? Not so much. I was exhausted by the time I took the step of hiring a COO and was at risk of running myself down. It took some time to realize that investing in a great team was essential for Zink Talent's long-term growth. People always say that if you're going to be a boss, you have to learn to delegate and "let go." Real talk: you also have to learn to let go of money!

- *Don't force it.* Entrepreneurs have a natural tendency to want to fix things and drive action at all times. Sometimes, though, the best thing you can do is *nothing*. I learned this in the early days of the COVID-19 pandemic, when business came to a standstill (which drove me crazy). I learned that you can't force things in business. Whether it's a client or an employee or a contract, sometimes the puzzle piece doesn't fit. When that happens, you've got to let it go and be OK with the unknown that follows.

- *Keep working on you.* There's this misconception that the boss can do whatever they want because they're calling the shots.

But when I became a boss, that's when I experienced some of my biggest growing pains yet—for example, as I learned my management style and worked on leading with kindness. I'd had the example of what *not* to do throughout my PR career. Breaking out of the mold I'd been "raised on" professionally required a commitment to self-improvement. Whatever stage of life you're in, personally or professionally, there's probably some area you can improve in.

Trying to write a single chapter about the growing pains Zink Talent (and I) faced over the years wasn't easy. This chapter only covers the highlights; if I detailed every little issue, I'd have an entire book. I think the biggest takeaway for myself has been knowing that the growing pains are always temporary. At the end of the day, a little discomfort is OK. As long as I have a roof over my head and I'm healthy, fuck it—the rest doesn't *really* matter in the grand scheme of things, right? I'm not saying that to be flippant or discouraging. It's just a little reminder (one I still have to give myself) that, if those growing pains start to get you down, some perspective may be needed. Remember what really matters, so that when you start to experience your own growing pains, you'll be able to inhale, breathe through the pain, and say, *I've got this.*

# CHAPTER 6

## From Zink's Point of View

After years as the CEO of Zink Talent, I've come to recognize that I was probably always meant to be my own boss. In my earlier PR days, I stood out—and not always in a good way. Even as a junior PR agent, I loudly shared my ideas, even if those ideas ruffled feathers. The most controversial point of view I ever had? Unpopular opinion number one: PR was dying, and influencers were the future. The PR veterans who had devoted their entire careers to the field didn't love hearing that.

Although I can't be 100 percent sure, I think that, on one occasion, my insistence on advocating for influencers over traditional PR media outlets actually contributed to me losing a job. This was toward the very end of my PR career. My intern days were well behind me, and I'd gathered experience at multiple agencies. I hadn't yet found the final agency I'd work for, the one that would actually encourage me to work with influencers. It was the agency right before that—*that* was the agency that fired me.

Even now, as a CEO with my own team, I can feel the sting of that firing. It *still* sucks to think about! And the memory is so fresh, whenever I think about it, it's like reliving it all over again.

*This is it. They're finally going to give me a promotion. And a much-needed raise.* I was thrilled. The higher-ups at the PR agency had called an impromptu meeting, and I was convinced that I was about to move up the corporate ladder, thanks in part to my out-of-the-box advocacy for influencers.

The agency I worked for at the time was well established but traditional; they wanted us to pitch *Vogue* and *Harper's Bazaar*. To them, influencers were a joke. To be fair, that's what most people at the time thought. But I wasn't so sure. I had been watching their follower counts tick up higher and higher and observed the way everyday people authentically connected with social media personas. I saw the potential impact influencers could have, addressing thousands every day to advocate for products they personally used and loved. So, I'd decided to start pushing the agency to get serious about influencers.

At the year-end holiday party, I'd cornered one of the senior leaders in the company and talked his ear off about the value of influencers—how they were shifting the "word-of-mouth" marketing landscape, how large their audiences were growing, how they were creating a sense of organic connection between companies and consumers. That annual company party was a boozy affair, and everyone was getting *lit*. I may have been a little bit tipsy (OK, I was definitely tipsy) when I cornered this fifty-five-year-old senior leader on the dance floor and told him, point-blank, "PR is dying. Influencers are the thing. We can't just pitch trad media anymore."

The impromptu meeting was held shortly after. I had high hopes. At the time, it didn't strike me as odd that my bosses wanted to have the meeting not *in* the office but at a brunch spot across the street. I remember it distinctly, because it was at 11 Howard, the hotel that infamous grifter Anna Delvey (allegedly?) conned out of some $30,000. I figured the bosses wanted to buy me breakfast to celebrate a promotion. Nice, right?

Not quite.

When I showed up, I was met by my immediate manager, my manager's boss, and a representative from human resources. You probably already see where this is going. By now, I know that a surprise appearance from HR is rarely a good thing. But back then, I didn't have a clue.

During that meeting, they dropped the ultimate f-bomb: *fired*. I was let go. The encounter had clearly been strategically planned off the premises; I'm not quite sure why. In case I made a scene, maybe. But I was so shocked, making a scene was the last thing on my mind. I was too surprised to even ask *why*.

The truth is, I still don't know why I was let go from that agency. The coworkers I talked to about it later couldn't name a reason either. The only thing I can think of, even now, is that my questioning the future of PR rubbed the wrong people the wrong way. Fair enough. I mean, I basically told them, "I don't believe in your business model; in fact, I think your whole industry is about to go up in flames." It's not exactly giving #teamplayer vibes.

Still, at the time, the firing was a shock. When I got the news, I was shaking—literally. I remember taking the paperwork they slid across the table to me, which outlined my dismissal and severance package, and telling them, "I'll need to have my attorney look this over." As if I had an attorney! I was in my mid-twenties and living in Manhattan on a $65,000 salary. Of *course* I didn't have a lawyer, and I'm sure they knew it.

Afterward, I couldn't bring myself to return to the office to get my things. I had to call my coworkers to bring my stuff out to me. My years of hard work ended with me slinking away with a box full of office supplies, like some cliché out of a movie or TV show.

I was heartbroken. Getting fired *sucks*. You feel like the world is ending. You feel like you screwed up. You feel like your career has been torpedoed. Your entire future has gone up in smoke before it's even really begun.

You know that cheesy saying, "When a door closes, a window opens"? Well, the next job I landed was with that *last* PR agency, the one that shared my opinion on influencers and hired me specifically to run an influencer vertical within their agency. Getting fired allowed me to move on to a role that was a better fit. Still, I was operating in an industry that was shifting rapidly under my feet.

In the years that followed, I had a front-row seat to the fall of traditional PR and, with it, the rise of the influencer era. It was a wild ride to be on—and it's what allowed me to start Zink Talent in the first place. Let's talk about it.

## The Rise of the Blogger: *Sex and the City* Goes *Gossip Girl*

When I was growing up, the vision I had of PR came from *Sex and the City*. There was Samantha Jones, running her own PR agency in NYC. On the other side, there was Carrie Bradshaw, writing her sex and dating column for a New York newspaper, a traditional media outlet. Both sides of the PR machine were represented. Traditional PR was all about getting clients visibility in those kinds of traditional print media.

With the rise of the internet and online publications, the focus shifted to online media, but it was still the big household names calling the shots. When I started PR in 2013, we were only dealing with traditional media. If one of our clients was showing a collection, we were going to Hearst Media and *Vogue, Harper's Bazaar, Complex, Esquire*— all the big names. People from those publications would come to a showing, view the collection, take notes, ask questions, and write up a review. It was stressful, because these professionals would give an honest critique. If they didn't like a designer's line, they'd say so. The PR agency and the designer would be holding their breath, hoping that the review would be good—but there were no guarantees. It's not like today, where brands give influencers money, the influencers wear the clothes and take a photo, and that's it. The environment back then felt more cutthroat.

The first signs of change came with the rise of the blogger. In 2007, *Gossip Girl* debuted, an entire TV show based on the musings of an anonymous blogger. I devoured the show in college, obsessing over the fashion just as much as the juicy storylines. When I got to New York years later, I felt like I was living my *Gossip Girl* dreams in real life. The fashions, the fast-paced city, the Manhattan backdrop. It was all there.

I'd also see famous faces at the PR events I worked, including John Legend, Future, Ryan Gosling, Emma Stone, Mary-Kate Olsen, and Brooke Shields. Seeing Sarah Jessica Parker made me feel like I was in *Sex and the City*. Sometimes, my celebrity interactions were quick, just checking them into an event. But if a celebrity was the face of an agency campaign, I'd get to work with them more closely, organizing and sitting in on media interviews to make sure the journalist asked all and only approved questions. For a twenty-something girl, it was very cool. I was shaking, to say the least.

The *Gossip Girl* effect was evident in my work life, too. Bloggers were on the rise. Around 2013, when I started in PR, they were becoming increasingly prevalent. These bloggers were basically early-stage "influencers" as we know them today. Their main selling point would be their blog, where they would post pictures of their fashions and write short blogs about them. They'd use their social media to push the blogs, posting images from their website on platforms like Instagram.

At this time, these bloggers weren't really getting paid; usually, they'd just get free clothes. The agencies I worked for from 2013 to 2015 would gift these online personalities fashions, but I don't remember working on any paid campaigns during that time. At most, the blogger would get an invite to a fashion week event or collection preview so that they could write a blog post about it, but we weren't paying them cash.

As online bloggers/influencers started populating the space and commanding more attention, it became increasingly difficult to pitch traditional media. When I started in PR, it was easy to pitch publications and get them to write about our clients. The loop between PR agencies and media outlets was uninterrupted. As PR agents, we had our roster of journalist contacts. We'd reach out to them when we had something new (and maybe take them out for a schmoozing lunch or two), and then they'd write something up for their publications.

Then, the media industry started getting subsumed by the internet. A lot of writers were being let go. The journalist contacts I'd nurtured for years faded. This wasn't an issue just for me but for many PR agents. Journalists were getting fired, job hopping, and going freelance. Many of them, sensing the difficult times ahead in traditional media, were leaving the business altogether.

The PR agents working on the front lines dealing with journalists saw the shift. However, the higher-ups in the agencies who weren't handling actual pitches were largely sheltered from the change. They weren't the ones writing journalists only to get automated *I'm no longer with this publication* messages. They weren't the ones being told that budgets had been slashed and space in the magazine was limited. They didn't see what was happening firsthand.

Meanwhile, as traditional media was giving way to the internet, social media was taking off. Instagram, the original app of choice for fashion bloggers to promote their websites, was evolving. Whenever a new app came out with an innovative idea, Instagram hopped on board. First, there was Snapchat; then, there was Instagram Stories. More recently, we've seen Instagram Reels come out in response to the popularity of TikTok. Around 2016, there was also the rise of the YouTube vlogger, which commanded a whole new level of attention. With social media advancing, the pressure on traditional media was even greater.

Again, my bosses in PR weren't seeing it (maybe they didn't want to). I'm not one to hold back, so I wasn't shy about flagging the changes. I'd tell the old-school agencies I worked for, "Hey, we need an influencer division." When my bosses got angry because media placements were waning, I'd try to explain: "Journalists are leaving. Magazines are shrinking. Budget cuts are happening. We can't make media placements like we once did."

Another issue was the rise of online fashion. Anybody could launch their own line and website, and as a result, the remaining fashion writers were overwhelmed by pitches. Unless you were a globally recognized brand, getting their attention was extremely challenging.

Again, the PR bosses weren't tuning into all of that. All they knew was they wanted media placements, and they weren't happy when those media placements didn't materialize. They would continually overpromise to clients and then get angry at the agents when they couldn't deliver on those unrealistic promises. That also contributed to what I perceived to be an increasingly toxic work environment in PR—and it hadn't been great to begin with!

Unpopular opinion number two: I feel like I got out of PR just in time. In 2018, when I started Zink Talent, influencer management was still a relatively new field. Sure, there were modeling agencies and talent agencies looking to expand into influencer management. But there weren't a lot of agencies focusing exclusively on influencers. I already had a foothold in the industry when fashion companies came around—which I'd say didn't happen until the COVID-19 pandemic. Yes, influencers had clout before that. But it wasn't until the pandemic that even the big, iconic brands finally gave in and, in many cases, became influencer-first. Traditional media, as we knew it, had lost her crown. Social media took the throne.

## Confessional: We Witnessed Samantha's Showdown with Traditional PR

*Jacob and Kaylee, Samantha's former coworkers*

*Jacob:* We all worked together at a PR agency in New York at a time when the industry was shifting. I was already on the social media side, but that part of the business was still very rudimentary.

*Kaylee:* The age of the influencer hadn't hit yet. Traditional press was still the gold standard, while influencers were this lower echelon. People who had been in the PR industry a long time were especially reluctant and somewhat skeptical to that being a possible shift. They didn't want to hear an entry-level PR girl telling them PR was dead and influencers were the relationships to prioritize.

*Jacob: Also*, the agency we worked for was based in the United Kingdom and run by a British founder. And the Brits really live and die by their press. If something wasn't getting picked up by the *Evening Standard*, for example, it didn't matter. There was also a bit of a US versus UK vibe, which added to the friction.

*Kaylee:* In general, there were underlying elements that toed the line of a toxic work culture. Arbitrary rules that I think relate to office hierarchy and the control that comes with it. Like, at one point, a group of junior people would go pick up lunch together every day. Then, a week later, seniority put a limit on the number of people who could get lunch at the same time.

*Jacob:* Yes, it was very hierarchical, which definitely created some internal barriers. The seniority structure was made very clear.

*Kaylee:* Right, and then I think when you had someone young and new to the industry like Samantha so strongly insisting on this new way of doing things, despite pushback, that was maybe seen as not respecting that hierarchy. It was sort of hypocritical, though, because the agency tried to create an environment that fostered open conversation and friendship. Weekly happy hours or, like, the Christmas party, you'd be drinking with your coworkers and your bosses would be sharing personal stories. There was a sense of comfort for everyone like, "Oh, I can speak freely here!"

*Jacob:* Which Samantha then did ...

*Kaylee:* That Christmas party is when she approached one of the senior leaders and basically said, "PR is dead, it's all about influencers." I remember her telling me they had a positive reaction that night but, given what happened almost immediately after, it's possible they felt it was a bit too bold.

*Jacob:* I think they took it personally.

*Kaylee:* She was fired not long after that.

*Jacob:* It came out of left field. They pulled her into an offsite meeting to do it. She texted me afterward–I remember she didn't even come back to the office to get her stuff. We had to run it out to her.

*Kaylee:* We were definitely surprised. It didn't make any sense. We had plenty of clients, the agency was doing well, and she was always doing her job.

*Jacob:* Right. I don't think she was ever ineffective or lacked work ethic. And the agency moved to a fancy new office in Dumbo shortly after that, so it's not like they were hurting for money.

*Kaylee:* We could never really figure out why she got let go. But after that, every time someone got pulled into an offsite meeting in *that* building, we all knew they were about to get fired.

*Jacob:* Yeah, she was a pioneer in that sense, too.

I'm friends with Jacob and Kaylee to this day, and we still talk about when I got fired. The exact reasons *why* remain a mystery. Either way, it's good to have friends who I can look back with on that day— and just laugh about it. What was so traumatic then doesn't look so horrifying now, because it helped set me on my current path.

# The Reality TV Age: Entering Our "Authentic" Era

Is PR as an industry dead? No. Is media dead? No. But both industries have changed. The PR world I worked in was both elite and elitist. Anna Wintour reigned supreme. I'd see her at industry events, always with her sunglasses on and an entourage in tow, and it was truly like seeing royalty. People would stop whatever they were doing when she entered a room. A hush would fall when she walked in—a mixture of respect, awe, and fear. Of course, Anna Wintour is still revered today, but she doesn't have the same chokehold on the fashion industry as she once did, because the entire PR, media, and fashion environment has changed.

Social media has leveled the playing fields in a lot of ways. Consumers aren't reliant on a few "expert" opinions from *Vogue* or *Harper's Bazaar*. The internet offers thousands of outlets for discovering fashion of all kinds, for all kinds of people. In many ways, the online world has served as an equalizer, leveling the playing field and allowing for greater diversity in fashion—both in terms of the clothes and who they're made for. We're seeing clothes and beauty products made for more varied body types, races, gender identities, and religions, which is awesome.

We're also seeing a shift toward greater authenticity. People don't want to only see picture-perfect supermodel types on their social feeds anymore. I mean, if we wanted that, we could have just stuck to the traditional media model, right? Consumers don't want to look at a 1990s supermodel wearing an outfit. Consumers want to look at someone with a body like *theirs*, not Naomi Campbell's or Kate Moss's, wearing the outfit. Understandably so!

I think the move toward authenticity we're seeing in social media is very cool. But here comes unpopular opinion number three: I also feel obligated to point out that the "authenticity" we're seeing is often being orchestrated. I've had brands get back to me and tell me the influencers I've pitched them are "too pretty." They want "everyday" or "normal" people. They will blatantly request a "curvy" girl or a "diverse" guy. Consumers have let the world know that representation matters, and brands are taking notice.

Alongside a shift toward authenticity, we're also seeing the trend of *de*-influencing, with social media personalities taking a stand against the excessive marketing and hyper-consumerism that have come to dominate the influencer landscape in the past years. People don't want to *feel* like they're being sold to. Of course, we all now know that influencers are selling stuff. The curtain on influencers was lifted long ago. We're well aware that this is modern-day marketing. When that twenty-year-old with the flawless skin recommends a certain skincare product to you, it's probably because she's getting paid for it. Influencer marketing has become so mainstream, there are now laws governing it. The rise of hashtags like #ad and #sponsored to acknowledge when content is paid for is a direct result.

All of this creates a more complicated landscape for companies looking to leverage influencers in their marketing. A few years ago, a brand would happily pay an influencer for a post just because that influencer had a lot of followers. They might throw $3,000 at an influencer for a single post, check that the post was done, and that was it. Everybody was happy.

That's no longer the case. We're dealing with more knowledge-able consumers. We're dealing with legislation. We're dealing with an increasingly flooded marketplace. As a result, brands have to be way more intentional about where they're putting their marketing dollars. That means the following:

- *Selecting the right influencers.* Follower count alone isn't enough. Brands need to confirm that the followers are real. They need to examine engagement. They need to review the influencer's audience to see if it aligns with the brand's target audience.

- *Clarifying marketing goals.* Brands also need to be clear about their goals and what return on investment (ROI) they're seeking. They have to think carefully about their intention. Do they want brand awareness? Increased sales? To launch a new product?

- *Giving influencers guidance.* Finally, when it comes to actually working with influencers, brands often need to provide guidance. They need to issue creative guidelines, brand guidelines, and talking points to the influencers they work with. After all, influencers aren't trained marketers or salespeople.

This creates a whole lot of extra burden on brand marketing departments. That's one reason brands work with companies like Zink Talent. We give them transparent, honest insights into our influencers, and we're able to advise on which of our influencers fit their audience and marketing intentions. It's kind of like matchmaking. We want to match the right brand with the right influencer. It's in our interests to get it right so that the brand sees the ROI they want and comes to us again in the future.

When we match influencers and brands, we're also looking at platforms. If you want to market to Gen Z, for example, you're probably going to want to go to TikTok. A successful TikTok campaign is going to look different from a successful Instagram campaign. TikTok posts get pushed down the feed so quickly; more frequent posts are needed, at least four a day, to make an impact. You also can't measure or track ROI on TikTok the same way you can on Instagram.

Social media can be a powerful marketing and advertising tool. But it requires more than simply having a pretty influencer put up a post to make it work for you. As CEO of Zink Talent, it's up to me to track the trends and sense the shifts in the marketplace.

## America's Next Top Model: What's Next in the World of Influencers?

What's next in the world of influencers? Real talk: even I can't know for sure! I got to where I am by anticipating the shifting media landscape. Being able to see trends coming down the pipeline has helped me succeed. Unfortunately, I don't have a crystal ball to see the future—but I have some ideas about where things are headed, and I'm adapting Zink Talent's offering accordingly.

I think the authenticity movement will continue—and become even more complicated, as people start to recognize the orchestrated authenticity I mentioned. TikTok opened the space for "everyday" people to make it big, with users tending to be less filtered, composed, and Facetuned compared with the earlier days of Instagram. People don't necessarily want to idolize some distant image of perfection; they want to meaningfully connect with the people they see online. The noise about "parasocial relationships," where followers develop one-sided relationships with an influencer, is a testament to that desire for connectivity.

Things are changing on the consumer side, too. Kids are getting their first smartphones and hopping onto social media younger and younger. To a ten-year-old, a twenty-five-year-old isn't going to resonate. They want to see someone their age (or close to it). We're seeing social media trending younger, and we're bringing on younger talent as a result. In fact, we recently brought our first underage influencer into the fold! Yes, his parents have to sign off on all of his deals—a first in a working relationship for me.

I'm also seeing more happening for guys on social media. Socials used to be dominated by pretty girls focused on fashion and beauty. Now, the gentlemen have entered the chat. Zink Talent has been stocking up its roster of male influencers accordingly. I can't wait to see how this new business niche unfolds going forward.

Looking even further into the future, there are also disruptive technologies that might affect the influencer space. Artificial intelligence (AI) is stirring up a lot of industries. There are some AI models already active on social media, mostly in the OnlyFans space (which isn't an area Zink Talent works with—no judgment, it's just not our niche)! Personally, I haven't seen AI influencers making much of a mark in fashion and beauty, but that's not to say it isn't possible. I do have a male model client who came on my podcast, *As Told by Zink*, and told me that some models he knew have been selling the rights to use their likenesses for AI. So, modeling seems to be impacted already. But given the way we're increasingly seeking authenticity and connection through social media, I don't think AI is going to take over yet.

But who knows? Maybe one day Zink Talent will sign its first AI-generated influencer. I try to keep an open mind and don't rule out any possibilities. Again, I'm always looking back on my PR career, which taught me a lot of great skills—but also taught me a lot of what *not* to do. I don't want to be like one of those outdated PR higher-ups who denied the rise of the influencer and failed to adapt in time to keep up.

For the moment, I want to focus on maintaining Zink Talent's credibility while staying on top of the ever-shifting landscape. Zink

Talent has established a solid reputation by now, one that I am determined to protect—we worked hard for it! For example, we do exclusive contracts, so our influencers secure deals only through us. They can't work with other agents or brands directly. This helps ensure that we are consistently delivering the quality that brands want, because we're taking care of all that research that I mentioned, like making sure the influencer's target audience matches the brand's.

Another big business move I made was to require all our talent to include the Zink Talent handle or Zink email in their bio. Similar to exclusive contracts, this is something I *only* asked of people once I felt the agency had the credibility to warrant the mention. I want brands to see Zink Talent on an influencer's profile and know, "Oh, this person is legit." That's the kind of power I want the Zink Talent name to have—and I think we're there. Brands know and respect us; they want to work with us. Maintaining that good reputation requires maintaining quality.

That quality starts with the influencers we work with, and I know Zink Talent wouldn't be anywhere without the *talent*. That's why I'm picky about who we sign—and by now, because of our reputation, I can afford to be picky! In the beginning, I was ready to sign *any*one, but now, I'm more discerning. We have about sixty influencers signed and continue to grow. I'd say we get DMs on Instagram every day from influencers wanting to be signed, on top of hundreds of website and email submissions every month. I review every submission personally; ultimately, we accept less than 5 percent.

I also seek out talent proactively—which comes naturally, because I love and spend a lot of time on social media! I still enjoy scrolling and devouring the fashion, beauty, travel, and people. If I think someone would be a good fit for Zink Talent, I'll reach out directly to set up an informational call. Above all, that genuine passion has allowed

me to succeed and stay relevant in an increasingly saturated market. I may be a thirty-something CEO now, but at heart, I'm still that same social-media-obsessed twenty-something girl, living the dream I voiced in that subway epiphany so many years ago. How cool is that?

# #Inspo: If You Don't Believe in Yourself, Why Should Anyone Else?

Recognizing the shifting media landscape in my later PR days was pivotal to my eventual shift to the social media space. When I started in PR, influencers were barely a thing, let alone influencer management. My role model was Samantha Jones, a traditional PR queen. There wasn't someone I could look at, in fiction or reality, who was doing influencer management. I had to pave my own path.

There are a few things I did that helped me succeed in my journey. Social media is such a rapidly changing field, but these are still core values I adhere to now, because I know I can't get complacent:

- *Keep your eyes and ears open.* Whatever industry you work in, whether it's social media or something else, odds are it's going to transform. New technologies may develop, trends may arise, and consumer demands may shift. Never stop learning about your field. Stay involved and up to date, and you'll stay relevant.

- *Adapt as needed.* When you see industry shifts, don't just watch them go by. Figure out how to adapt to them. You don't want to be left behind because you didn't evolve with the evolving world.

- *Go forward with conviction.* Adapting to industry changes often means being one of the first to do something. Being one of the first can help you succeed. But it will also result in backlash. Stick to your guns. Believe in your vision, even if those around you don't. Because, hey, if *you* don't believe it, why should anyone else?

Confession: change can be kind of scary. I was definitely nervous when changes came my way; seeing the PR industry crumbling wasn't fun! The changes in media, PR, and the world of influencers have been overwhelming at times. But change has also been the secret to my success. It can also be the secret to yours.

# CHAPTER 7

## The Ins and Outs of Influencer Management

I take a deep breath, close my eyes, and gulp it back. *Ugh.* I wrinkle my nose and try not to gag.

No, it's not a tequila shot.

It's a wheatgrass shot.

This is me now: hitting the SoulCycle studio, taking Ryder for a walk, getting my green juice. Staying in on Friday nights. I know. Look, if you had told me in my twenties that I would one day be happy to stay in on a Friday, I would have laughed in your face. But that's where I'm at now. Growing up—it gets all of us. Trust me.

I can't believe I'm this girl now, but I don't regret it for a second. I also don't regret the partying days of my twenties. I mean, I wasn't *always* like this.

For a few years in NYC, I really *was* living the *Gossip Girl* life, including one very pivotal part: I basically dated the real-world Chuck Bass. I'll keep his name out of this and simply say he is the heir to a major publishing fortune and his wedding (to a girl he dated after we were involved—no overlap or salacious scandals) was featured in *Vogue* magazine.

I met "my" Chuck Bass when I was twenty-three, at the height of my PR-girl party days, and going to 1 Oak, *the* night club of the moment in the city, religiously. It was my church, except I'd go every Friday night instead of every Sunday morning. Actors, athletes, musicians—I saw more than one famous face there.

But there was *one* face in particular that jumped out at me—*his*. I was dancing and locked eyes with this guy and he just kind of smirked at me. He was smoking a cigarette, which he handed to me to take a drag, which I did (I know, I know—I never was a true smoker and would not touch a cigarette today; don't judge me too harshly, please). Maybe it was the nicotine. Maybe it was that sexy half-smile of his. Maybe it was his quiet confidence—the kind of quiet confidence that comes with old money—I was *hooked*. We spent the rest of the night dancing together, him in a suit that probably cost thousands of dollars and me in my Rent the Runway dress with my Forever 21 bag. I remember the buckle on that bag was tarnished, a clear red flag screaming "Cheap!" and I was so worried he'd notice. Turns out, he didn't care about my bag.

After that night, we kept seeing each other. It was never serious—we usually caught each other between one or the other's relationships—which was fine by me. It was just fun. We'd have a big night out and end up at his Upper East Side penthouse, where I'd wake up the next morning with an exhilarating feeling of *What is my life?!* plus, usually, a hangover.

It was silly, wild, and totally unserious. Perfect for that era of my life. The PR party-girl era. I lived her and I loved her—and now she's a cherished part of my past.

As I entered my CEO era, I realized that lifestyle wasn't working for me anymore. The parties, the unserious guys, the hangovers *after* the parties—all of that interfered with my clarity. When I started Zink Talent, I became more conscious of both my mental and physical health. I became even more dedicated to my well-being when I moved to LA. Now, writing this book, I'm in yet another transitional period and renewing my dedication to my health—working out more, eating better, and drinking only on occasion (and, when I do, mindfully).

Part of that shift comes down to what I do. I want to continue to take Zink Talent to new heights. I can't maintain clarity of vision and dedicate myself fully to that vision if I don't have a clear head myself. I can't be lying in bed horizontally with a pounding headache all day Sunday and crawling out of the weekend barely ready to face the Monday.

As a boss, I need to be switched on all the time. This is especially true in the field of influencer management, where everyone is online pretty much 24/7. Anti-gatekeeping tip number one: if you want to make it in social media, you've got to do the same.

# Influencers and Their Managers: All On, All the Time

For better or worse, we all have access to social media constantly. Wherever you are, whatever you're doing, all you have to do is grab your phone and start scrolling to lose yourself in that world. Is it always good for us? Probably not. I'll give you some real talk on some of the dangers I've noticed working in the social media world in chapter 9 (plus, what Zink Talent is trying to do to tackle those dangers).

But for now, that is a reality I can't escape: my work requires me to be on socials a lot. I love it and can scroll for hours, don't get me wrong. The point I'm trying to make is that I'm constantly switched on. A lot of people use aimless scrolling as a break from work; when you're in social media, the scrolling is part of the work. You're constantly keeping an eye out for new trends, new influencers, new sounds—whatever the case may be.

As the head of an influencer management agency, it's my responsibility to be aware of those things. I expect the same of my agents. We need to know the landscape so that we can help our clients navigate it.

That's the other thing: our clients are also plugged in 24/7. There's a common misconception that influencers live glamorous lives, always on extravagant trips, eating at expensive restaurants, attending splashy events. While that *can* be true for big names, the reality is that most influencers are, more than anything else, creating content—often at home, sometimes in sweatpants. Anti-gatekeeping tip number two: it's not as glamorous as you might think.

This has become especially true with TikTok. Being a successful influencer on TikTok means consistently making a *lot* of content. They are constantly creating. If they're a beauty influencer, it could be a "Get Ready with Me"; if they're a fashion influencer, it could be an "Outfit of the Day" or a "Fit Check" video.

Making all that content takes time, dedication, and attention to detail—especially when you're collaborating with brands like the ones Zink Talent works with. The brands have strict guidelines that the influencers need to follow. For every partnership, the influencer gets photo guidelines and talking points they need to cover. If the influencer doesn't abide by the brand's content creation guidelines, the brand will request a reshoot—and the creator has to start from zero.

Influencers only have a tiny percentage of creativity in the entire process. This is especially true for larger globally known brands like

Nike or Adidas. They want to make sure any content affiliated with them is true to their brand and mission statement.

At the same time, brands want the influencer to be unique and authentic. Because that's why we like influencers, right? Super scripted, robotic posts usually flop. People want content that's organic and real; they don't want to feel like they're being sold to. Sure, it's no secret that social media is basically a giant ad by now—but we still want the *feeling* of authenticity.

The thing is, it's not always easy for an influencer to deliver "real" when they're also trying to abide by pages of guidelines. For example, a skincare or vitamin brand is going to want the creator to highlight key ingredients in the product—but the creator still has to talk about those ingredients in a natural way while also sounding enthusiastic. It's a lot like being an actor.

So, what's *my* role in all of this? What is Zink Talent doing behind the scenes while our influencers are busy creating content? We keep pretty busy ourselves.

# The Role of the Influencer Manager

Zink Talent is basically the touchpoint between the influencer and the brand. We handle all communication between the two. A big part of our job is pitching. We are exclusive with all our clients, so we want to make sure they are getting the best collaborations. We pitch them out constantly, combing through our database of brands and PR agencies to find opportunities that are a good fit. In some cases, a brand will reach out to the influencer directly, in which case the influencer will connect the brand to *us*, and we then negotiate a deal on the influencer's behalf.

If a brand is interested in an influencer, they'll ask for their insights and rates. Insights consist of back-end information about the influencer, like their audience demographics, reel views, story views, and TikTok engagement—everything on the back end of the social media profile that the public can't see. These details matter to brands. Say a brand of yoga-wear for women wants to work with a female influencer. If that influencer's audience is 90 percent male, she's not a strong contender for that brand, which is targeting women.

Along with the insights, we'll also send the influencer's rates. Rates vary according to the individual, brand, platform, and content type. Whenever possible, we try to sell bundles. At this point, the agent's job is basically that of a salesperson. When you are pitching an influencer to a brand, you want to hype them up as much as possible to justify the rate. As with any sales-oriented industry, upselling is a smart move—something we accomplish with bundles. So, I might tell a brand, "OK, you can have one reel for $3,000, or we can do three reels for $7,000."

In some cases, brands want to syndicate an Insta reel to TikTok or vice versa. In that case, instead of charging them the full rate for the reel plus the full rate for the TikTok, I'll give them a discounted rate that allows for syndication. So, they can use the same video on both platforms—and the influencer only has to create one piece of content. Multipurpose content like that, as well as multiple content pieces, usually gets the brand a better ROI as well. Upselling isn't just about making more money; it's about ensuring the brand is happy with the outcome (which can then mean more business later).

Hopefully, the brand will like the influencer's insights and agree to some kind of bundle. Let's say that brand of yoga-wear for women wants to work with one of Zink Talent's female influencers. She's got a strong female following, in line with the brand's target audience, and they've agreed to her rate—one reel syndicated to TikTok for $5,000.

At this point, Zink Talent circles back to the influencer via chat (email takes too long). We present the influencer with the opportunity details—the brand, deliverable, and rate—and ask if they want to pass or confirm. If they confirm, we add the job to our database of ongoing collaborations and create a brand-facing folder for all relevant materials, including the creative brief and, later, the content. If they pass, we let the brand know (sugarcoating the answer as needed to preserve future possibilities).

We then also confirm the deal with the brand, and they send a contract. Zink Talent reviews the contract. We're basically just trying to make sure the brand isn't sneaking anything extra into the contract. For example, they might try to sneak in advertising or website usage, which they have to pay extra for. We usually go back and forth a few times before the contract is signed.

Only *then* do we get to the creative stuff. Let's continue with the example of the women's yoga-wear brand. The brand might then send a look book for the influencer to check out. The influencer will pick three outfits. We'll then share the influencer's selects and shipping address with the brand, and the brand will send the goods via registered mail (traceable). Once the influencer gets the gear, the deadlines kick in. So, the brand might say, "We need content to review by January 15 and we want to take it live by January 18."

On the Zink Talent side, we're compiling all this information into the relevant folder and updating the Google Doc so that the influencer can quickly see their deadlines and all the information they need, such as the brief and content guidelines. When the influencer has created their content, they'll upload it into the fitting folder (e.g., we'd create content folders for separate deliverables for TikTok versus Reels).

The brand then gets the chance to review the content and can request edits or a reshoot. We share that feedback with the influencer. Once the content is approved and finalized, it can go live. Zink Talent then lets the brand know it's live and grabs insights from the post within twenty-four hours so that we can show the brand how successful it was. Our influencers rarely alert us when they're posting, so we have to scan their accounts regularly to grab the insights. Exactly when it is best for them to post depends on everything from location to target audience. You don't want to push out your best content when your target audience is asleep!

When we share the insights with the brand, we also invoice them. Zink Talent has someone who handles accounting and chases invoices. We do have to chase a lot for payments, and the payments are frequently late, so it's definitely worth having a dedicated person on top of it. We do also have an attorney connected to the agency whom we bring in if a brand doesn't pay and is nonresponsive. That rarely needs to happen, though! Once Zink Talent is paid, we take our cut—and then we pay our client, the influencer.

Yes, we do take a cut of the influencer's pay from each brand deal. But our clients know it's worth it. They don't have to deal with pitching, negotiating, reviewing contracts, and chasing payments. All they have to do is say yes or no when we come to them with an offer—and then, if they say yes, create the content in line with the brief they're given.

Our influencers also benefit from our database of contacts. Trying to pitch a major brand like Nike or Alo Yoga as an independent influencer is tough. Zink Talent has strong connections and a good reputation, which makes closing deals easier.

I actually prefer to work with influencers who have "done it alone" already, because I know they understand how much work Zink

Talent does for them. I tell them, "I want you to learn your business before coming on with me. I want you to have gone through at least ten brand deals from start to finish—negotiating, contracts, payment. Because then you'll understand your business fully before handing it off to someone else." I want influencers to be knowledgeable so that they understand what we do all day and why we are worth the commission percentage cut.

There is also a lot that we do that we *don't* get paid for but help organize anyway, such as events, brand meetings, travel opportunities, trade partnerships, and gifting—the list goes on. We only get paid a commission from the brand deals, but we are happy to do these extras for our clients to help them level up and get their name out there— and hopefully the efforts lead to a paid partnership with the brand or agency. The last thing I want is for a client to underappreciate what we do or feel resentful because they think the agency's cut isn't warranted.

# Finding a Soul Purpose in the Social Media World

I'll be the first one to admit it: most of my work is emails and contracts! It is *not* that glamorous working in influencer management. That said, it's not all me behind a laptop screen 24/7. We also attend brand meetings, join our influencers for events, and network to seek out new opportunities for our clients. That said, a lot of things that were previously in person are now handled online; the pandemic was a turning point in that respect.

And, again, the life of an influencer is not necessarily as glamorous as it might seem. Yes, there are the @Haleyyhaylee powerhouses who attend red carpet events and meet celebrities. That's simply not the reality for most of the industry. You're probably *not* going to get flown to Europe in a private jet or get an all-access pass to NYFW or be gifted a free Birkin. A lot of the "glamorous" things you see influencers doing they are paying for themselves. They may not be getting sponsored to go to the fancy restaurants, shops, or vacation destinations, but they can do so on their own dime. And that's pretty cool too, in my opinion.

That said, rates have gone down over the past decade as brands tend to spread the wealth. They'd often rather work with *more* influencers rather than allocating huge budgets to just a few. I want to be really clear about this point, because I see stories where people quit their day jobs to try to become influencers and I just want to say, please, don't—*unless* you have security. That security could be a partner or parent who's willing to support you, for example, or other streams of established income.

I am obviously all for taking a risk—Zink Talent was a risk! But as a marketing/management agency, I can pivot, whereas creators can't always. A lot of people become irrelevant because they don't want to try new trends, adapt their content to what's current, or be on new platforms. I've seen it happen to more than one millennial influencer.

On top of that, not only are the rates lower than they once were, but the competition is fiercer than ever. In the TikTok era, we've all seen how really anybody can go viral, and that fast flash of fame can be enough to make people think they've got a career in social media ahead of them. But think about all the viral videos you and your friends send back and forth every week—probably every day. Are all of those people who have gone viral going to make a living off of social media now? Probably not. TikTok has given people the opportunity to become accidental influencers. Is that always sustainable? Nope.

I'm not saying that to be discouraging. But I promised you, I'd be real with you!

There is one last word of caution I'll give to anyone who is thinking of working in the influencer space: beware the lack of soul purpose.

I've seen many influencers go from being excited about the business to feeling a lack of purpose—and eventually burning out as a result. Real talk: social media does not provide fulfillment. In the beginning, it's fun—you're making a lot of money, working with brands you love, building a following where people are engaging with you. You feel like a mini celebrity.

But fast-forward five years, and that sparkle will start to fade. You probably *won't* answer every DM or reply to every comment. You probably *won't* get all hyped up because a certain brand wants to work with you. And that's when you start not only losing motivation but also questioning your purpose.

I've seen countless influencers hit this wall, where they're like, "Yes, this is my income and I'm grateful for the opportunity to earn a living this way, *but …*" And they often don't know how to finish that sentence. They can't quite articulate what's missing. In my opinion, it's often the soul purpose.

One way that influencers find their spark again is by creating their own brand or pursuing their own business opportunity. They might enter into a collaboration with an existing brand, like Revolve. Or, they might start their own company altogether (this is something that a lot of beauty influencers do, starting makeup or skincare lines). Some influencers will also pursue other creative avenues, like a podcast. Often, these endeavors are what bring them fulfillment again. And that's ultimately what we're all looking for, right?

Anti-gatekeeping tip number three: whether you pursue social media or another path, don't forget your soul purpose.

# #Inspo: Are You Ready to Go All IN-fluencer?

Whether you have dreams of being an influencer or are interested in influencer management, there is money to be made in social media. I am *not* one to gatekeep, and I hope some of the things I've talked about in this book can help you on your path.

If you want to chase the dream, there are a few things I'd keep in mind:

- *Get obsessed and stay obsessed.* Whether you're working behind the scenes or in front of the camera, you have to be on Instagram and TikTok every day—and you have to follow a ton of influencers. I don't even hire interns unless they eat, sleep, and breathe social media. You have to know the people, trends, and conversations of the moment.

- *Accept that there will be mundane moments.* A lot of my job is writing emails. I have days where I don't do much else. I also have days where I'm accompanying an influencer to a brand event and my workday consists of eating, drinking, and mingling. But most days I'm behind my laptop. My influencers likewise are mostly working from home, creating content, often in their sweatpants. Yes, social media can pay well and provide access to fun opportunities and interesting people. But there's more to it than that.

- *Don't forget about your soul purpose.* Social media can be an amazing industry to work in. But is it your soul purpose? If you do decide to pursue this path, don't forget about that. Maybe your soul purpose lies within the social media space.

Maybe it lies somewhere else. Either one is OK. Just try to find something that fulfills you; a soul purpose will do that.

Whatever path you take in social media or beyond, create a clear vision for yourself. And, most important, take care of yourself! I'm definitely *not* trying to cram my healthy new lifestyle or my spirituality down your throat. I can only share my story and what has worked for me, and a big part of that was taking better care of myself. That allowed me the energy to articulate and manifest my vision. And if social media has taught us anything, it's that we can all indulge in a little self-care now and then, right?

# CHAPTER 8

# Building a Team That Has Your Back

"Remember that guy I dated who made me have a shared calendar with him?!"

"OMG, so he could track every minute of your day! We were genuinely concerned at one point."

"Yeah, glad he's history—he was *so* controlling."

"I'm going to need another glass of rosé if we keep talking about this."

"Um, make it another *bottle*, because if we're talking bad dates, remember the time I threw up on the guy?"

"YES!"

Ensue cackles of glee and the clinking of wine glasses. No, it's not a girl's night out. It's an episode of my podcast, *As Told by Zink* (hint: it's the "Zink after Dark" episode, if you want to hear me and my girlfriends reveal all).

When I was growing up, I never dreamed of having a podcast. Podcasts didn't even exist yet! But a few years ago, I felt like I might have a story to tell.

A story about finding my path in work.

A story about finding my way in love.

A story about finding, well, myself, to be honest.

The *As Told by Zink* podcast was born. It's a place where I can share my real, authentic self and, maybe, give people some inspiration or useful information while I'm at it, whether it's about dating or business. Maybe the podcast was born in part because I was seeking some larger soul purpose—some way to give back.

Now, I try to go to my podcast studio in LA once a week to record—and I'm rarely alone. Usually, I have a guest on. Sometimes, it's an influencer or someone else in the social media space. But just as often, it's a friend or a work contact—or a work contact who became a friend.

Over the years, I have managed to build an amazing team of people around me, both in my professional and personal life. These people *have my back*. I know I can count on them for the fun times—and when the tough moments hit. That is truly more valuable than any financial or professional success, and it is something I wish for everyone.

How do you go about building a team that's got your back, in life and at work? Let's talk about it.

## Building a Team at Work

When people interview me, they inevitably ask something along the lines of, "What is the key to your success?" And I've always had the same answer: the key to my success is finding a team that does the work just as well as me, or even better. There are a few hacks that I believe allow me to work with the best of the best.

Team-building hack number one: all remote, all the time. From the start, I operated Zink Talent remotely. I'm not saying I pioneered work remote, but I definitely did it before the pandemic. When I was working at PR agencies, I knew *only* office life. The expectation was that you did not leave your desk until your boss left their desk. It made so many parts of life, from going on dates to squeezing in a workout, so hard—especially for an eager young professional trying to be out on the town!

When I started Zink Talent, I never had an office space or insisted my employees be located in any particular city. The entire team was distributed. It's still that way today. I have agents working everywhere from LA to New York and San Diego. While I realize that a remote environment isn't possible in every field, I think it can be hugely beneficial when it is possible. Plus, it lets you connect with the most talented, motivated people you can find. Isn't that who you want on your team?

Traditional corporate hierarchies are another thing I have always been determined to avoid at Zink Talent. Beyond me and Carly (respectively, CEO and COO), everyone in the company has always operated as an agent. I don't do that bullshit of senior versus junior agents, because from what I saw in my PR days, those roles usually did the same tasks. Like when I got promoted from an intern to a junior agent at my first agency job, I was expected to keep doing my intern tasks while still doing agent tasks. I didn't want that for my team. We're all agents. We all have clients we manage. We all have collaboration deals we close. And we all get a cut of the deals we close. End of story.

Of course, trusting agents with that responsibility means training them. I've already mentioned my hands-on approach to training agents. Even now as CEO I haven't delegated that task to anyone else in the company. I still take the time to sit with every intern and personally show them the ropes.

This brings me to another valuable point: I still work with interns regularly, precisely *because* I can train them from zero—and I often hire out of my intern pool. While I don't exclusively hire internally, it's proven valuable in creating a bonded team that I can trust—and I do not underestimate that! After witnessing the backstabbing, snarky ways of the cutthroat PR scene in my twenties, I do *not* want to create that kind of toxic environment at Zink Talent.

That's why I also try to show appreciation for my team whenever I can. I make a point of celebrating our wins together, as a team, *openly*. In the PR world, accolades were rarely given. When they *were* given, they were absorbed by the top. The junior employees never got recognition, even if they were the ones doing the work that reaped the reward (say a mention on a magazine cover). I make sure to celebrate my team members' wins openly, giving credit where credit is due. If an agent secures an amazing partnership, for example, I'll celebrate them in our team group chat so that everyone knows about it.

Of course, I show my appreciation in other ways, too. After all, we all love words of affirmation, but we also love to get spoiled. That's why I regularly fly everyone on my team to a destination so that we can celebrate our successes together in style. The team has met up everywhere from NYC to Malibu to Nashville. We spend two to three days together. I set up some fun activities for us during the day and then treat everyone to swanky dinners in the evenings. It's a great way to reward my team while also giving them a chance to bond over some cool new experiences.

I encourage the team to find other opportunities to bond as well. We have a Zink Talent book club that meets (remotely) once a month, for example. One time, a couple of agents pitched me the idea of a pasta night. They organized an online pasta-making class, and we shipped out boxes with the basic supplies and some Zink merch to the whole team. Then we had this Italian chef show us how to make the pasta, with everyone tuning in from home. I'm happy to foot the bill for things like that, whether it's buying the team some books or paying a private chef. It's a chance for me to show my gratitude and for all of us to come together.

Team-building hack number two: show your appreciation. Is it necessary that I fly my team to meet once or twice per year? No. However, I think it's important to cherish your people. I want to show my team I care and thank them for their hard work. With getaway trips and exclusive events and lavish meals, I can show my very real gratitude and encourage them. And that keeps the momentum of Zink Talent going.

I previously had difficulty parting with my hard-earned money before making my first hire, thinking that paying someone else from Zink Talent's earnings meant less for me. Over the years, I've moved away from that limiting belief about money and developed an abundance mindset. Recognizing that there is always more to be had makes generosity come easily.

Plus, I truly believe that if you're taking care of people and treating them right, that will come back to you in abundance. That applies in my personal and my professional life. When I give people gifts, it's not about showing off. I genuinely get excited about giving people gifts (maybe it's my love language). And when I exercise that generosity, I also feel like it's seen by the universe (I know, I know, here I go with some of my woo spiritual stuff again). But truly, I feel like the universe *sees* me and is like, "Oh, she doesn't have a limiting belief that her money will run out. She's buying things for herself and for others with the mindset of *More money will come.* Let's send some her way." Shifting from a scarcity to an abundance mindset has been a game changer for me.

That's not to say it's all rainbows and sunshine. I'm human and I still make mistakes. And my team is composed of real people, with all their emotions and faults and ups and downs. I've had to learn to walk the fine line of being a friendly boss without becoming best friends with my employees. At the end of the day, I still need them to respect me. At the same time, I want them to be happy.

# Confessional: I'm an Influencer Talent Agent

*Zoe, Agent, Zink Talent*

I've been with Zink Talent since 2021–and I actually started out as the agency's social media manager, handling Instagram. But I wanted to do more, so one day, I approached Samantha about being an agent. The thing about Samantha is, if you work hard and show you want it, she'll give you a shot. She agreed to give me a trial run. And it worked out! I've been an agent ever since then (although I still handle Samantha's socials). Being able to grow within the team has been amazing.

My average day involves a *lot* of communication. I'm emailing clients every morning, letting them know what's in the works, what meetings I have scheduled for them, and what relationships I'm trying to kick off for them. At the same time, I'm responding to inbound emails and pitching out my clients. I also work with my clients on developing long-term game plans for their careers. There are also days where I attend events with clients or go to lunch with PR agencies (I'm based in New York). But most of my days are emails and calls.

For anyone wanting to get into influencer management, you've got to be ready to work in a fast-paced environment. Strong communication is also important. A lot can get lost in translation when a brief goes from a brand to the agency to the influencer. As the agent, it's my job to make sure *nothing* gets lost in translation.

I'd say it's also important to have a positive attitude and just be friendly. You don't want to have a cold, transactional relationship with your influencers; they don't want to feel like you're looking at them like they're dollar signs. I really care about my influencers and their growth and genuinely want to see them succeed. That also means keeping an eye on the industry as a whole. You have to 100 percent know where the industry is moving and pick up on trends quickly. That's how you'll be able to help your clients succeed.

I love Zoe's story because it epitomizes that "go get it" attitude that I embrace myself. She wanted to try a new role at Zink Talent, and, because I trusted her, I was happy to let her give it a try. And it all worked out—proof that you should always ask for what you want.

# Building a Team in Life

I don't fit the mold of what most people envision when they think *CEO*. I think plenty of C-suite executives would be wary of spending a full weekend getaway with their team, for example, or would shy away from sharing stories about their dating life on a podcast.

Here's the thing: I don't *want* to be a traditional CEO. I think younger professionals, millennials and Gen-Zers, are moving away from strict delineations between work and private life. It's OK to let the professional blend with the personal. I mean, of course there are limits! But weaving work into everyday life has its benefits.

In influencer management, it's sort of inevitable that work intersects with your private life. One reason for that is that you always have to be switched on and tuned in. I have clients around the world, so there is never a time of day when I'm not getting emails or text messages. My friends know that my phone *will* be on the table when we're out to dinner—and there is a chance I may need to pick it up to shoot off a quick text to a client or to email a brand.

Much of this approach stems from the industry I'm in and Zink Talent's remote-work policy (I imagine it's easier to leave work behind when it's confined to an office). But a big part of it is also that I *want* it that way. I'm big on weaving work into everyday life, because I don't want to "live for the weekends," and I don't want my team to, either.

I feel like when we strictly assign work from Monday to Friday, 9:00 a.m. to 5:00 p.m., and fun to the weekends only, we are losing out on a lot of life. I always tell my team, "I don't expect you to be at your desk all day. Go get a coffee. Take your dog for a walk. Sign up for a yoga class mid-day." I trust them to work when, where, and how they want, as long as the work gets done. This also opens up other freedoms to them, like being able to travel while working, without needing to use up vacation days. Of course, people take vacation days as well—I'm just saying, it creates even more opportunities, thanks to the extra flexibility it affords.

And I practice what I preach. I recently flew to Australia and spent three weeks there. I brought my laptop with me and was able to do my work from there while also getting to explore this amazing new place. When work is woven into everyday life like that, I think there's less dread around it as a whole. You're not just working toward the weekend or the next vacation. You can have bits and pieces of the weekend or vacation vibe any time you choose.

At least, that's my take. I'm sure this approach is *not* for everybody. In Zink Talent's case, it has served us well. So that's my team-building hack number three: weave work into everyday life. Because I definitely do *not* want my team suffering from the Sunday Scaries at the end of every weekend.

# #Inspo: Who's Got *Your Back?*

Zink Talent has been such a fulfilling endeavor for me—and it's taken me a while to figure out *why*, exactly. It's not the money (although that's nice). It's not that I get to make scrolling part of my job (also nice). This sounds so cheesy, but it's the people. I find fulfillment in this because of the community I've created—from my clients to my employees, I truly care about them. Even when I was in PR, my favorite part of the work was always the people, and I'm still close with some coworkers from my PR days now.

Over the years, I've built a team that's got my back, both at work and outside of work. Here's how I did it:

- *Invest in your team.* There are many ways to invest in your team. It doesn't have to be financial. Time is a simple factor—like the way I take time to train the interns at Zink Talent myself. But it's also simply about putting time into relationships, including friendships. If you've ever worked in a full-time job and had that coveted work bestie, you probably got super close with them, right? Think about how much time you spent with them! Forty hours a week, at least. You've got to put time into relationships. That's how strong connections are forged.

- *Show your gratitude.* I can't stress this one enough. When you've got people on your team, whether that's in work or life, show your appreciation! It doesn't have to be some lavish, expensive present. It can be a small gesture, like getting them their favorite coffee. It can be as simple as *telling* them. Write them a note, if you want to. Or just send them a meme you know they'll love. It's those little moments that make us feel appreciated.

- *You've got to trust.* When you've got your team, trust them. I trust my employees to get the job done without me hovering over their shoulders. I trust my friends will be there for me in good times and bad. This also requires trusting yourself— trust that *you* made the right decisions when you picked the people for your team. After all, you picked them for a reason.

I bet if you think about it right now, you can name some people who have your back. It could be your friends. It could be your work bestie. It could be your dog (I know Ryder is my ride-or-die). It could be your freaking parents! The point is, there are people who will have your back in this world. That's your team. Cherish them.

# CHAPTER 9

## It's Still Unwritten

*I wonder if he liked the last photo I posted.* I open Insta and to see if the hunky Australian guy I've been exchanging "likes" with for the past few hours has given my last picture a heart. *He did!*

Cue my fluttering heart. I don't even know this guy or how he found me! I decide to do what any boss babe who wants to take control of her own destiny would do.

I slide into his DMs.

I've always been an alpha female, so making the first move doesn't scare me. But what should I say?! Figuring out that first step is terrifying, to be honest. Luckily, I have a team of social media experts at my fingertips—so I consult the team at Zink Talent.

"Should I just say 'Hi'?"

The tribunal immediately assures me that this is the lamest opener ever. After some serious debating, my opener to the mysterious Aussie hunk halfway across the world is this: "When are you going to be in LA next?" Direct. Simple. And scary as hell to send.

But then.

He responds right away (*squeal*).

Flash forward a few months, and I'm in an online, long-distance relationship with a guy I've never even met in person. Just like I never anticipated becoming a CEO, it's another role I never, *ever* thought I'd end up in.

# Finding a Soulmate

After that first DM, B. and I exchanged messages for a bit before moving on to FaceTime—and that was when I felt it for the first time. This soul connection I'd never felt with any partner previously. We talked about entrepreneurship and spirituality and our histories and our hopes and dreams—all of it.

This was summer. By October of that year, he was visiting me in LA. I was so anxious; later, he told me I couldn't stop chattering in the car from LAX airport to my house. It was definitely the nerves. We had an amazing few weeks in LA—we went to a Clippers game, visited Disney and Universal Studios, and even carved pumpkins for Halloween. He also met my friends—and the number one guy in my life, obviously, my dog Ryder.

When B. left, he asked if I'd be up for visiting him in Australia. Two weeks later, I was on a plane. I flew to Gold Coast to visit him and meet his family. After that, we met in Mexico to attend a friend's wedding. It was a whirlwind. Eventually, we decided that it made the most sense for him to move to LA and strike the "long-distance" label off our relationship.

And that is how social media led me not only to a job I love but also to a man I love.

Finding someone who truly "gets" me has allowed me to see how wrong the people I dated previously were for me. A lot of the trouble came from my alpha female tendencies. I like to lead and take charge, and I've found out (the hard way) that a lot of guys *say* that they want a strong woman but when they're actually confronted with one, they change their minds.

There is also a financial component to it; some guys can be intimidated by a financially independent woman, especially if she makes more than them. I personally don't care if I earn more than my partner, and I also don't mind covering more in a relationship when it comes to things I want to do, like taking a fancy trip. I am happy to pay for experiences we can share together, knowing they are memories we will cherish. But money issues, coupled with my girl boss attitude, have led to friction in the past.

I remember shortly after I moved to LA, I dated a guy who consistently left all the planning to me. I was always coming up with fun stuff for us to do together! Then, the one time I left the planning to *him*, I found him browsing … Groupon. Don't get me wrong, I have no shame taking advantage of a Groupon promotion. But I was thinking something more romantic—like a helicopter ride over LA (in the vibe of *Fifty Shades of Grey*. If you've seen it, you can probably hear that Ellie Goulding song "Love Me Like You Do" in your head right now).

I wanted the helicopter ride. So, I booked it. And I paid for it. When I told the guy, he was clearly uncomfortable; I remember him awkwardly asking me how much it cost. The fear in his eyes was real; this was not a date that he wanted to go fifty-fifty on!

Confession: I lied. I told him that I'd gotten the helicopter ride as a perk of my job. I never admitted that I'd just paid for it in full, outright, with my own money. Amusing as it is to look back on my little white lie now, it also makes me sad that I felt like I had to squash down who I was, concealing my professional accomplishments and financial success.

Now that I've met someone who I have that real soul connection with, I don't feel that way. I actually think that the fact that B. and I met over social media helped us find that spark—that soul connection. And it's in that connection, in that safe space it gives me, that I've been able to get in touch with a more feminine side of myself I never could before. B. does things like open car doors for me, and I *love* it. Words I never thought I'd say!

It took me a long time to figure it out, but I finally realized that what matters is feeling a soul connection with somebody. Can you go deep and *really* talk about profound things? Can you fall in love with somebody's personality, their soul, before you've even touched them? If you don't have that, you're not going to make it. At least, that's what I think.

Here's the other thing I've learned: you will not find that soul connection if you don't make space for it. If you are afraid of being alone and settle for something "good enough," that person is taking up space in your life—space, time, and energy. Until you make space for the soul connection, you won't find it. And then who knows where you'll find it. It might even be in your DMs.

# Finding a Soul Purpose

Social media has given me so much in life. It's allowed me to build a business I'm passionate about. It's been essential to my financial success. It's even brought me love. But the most important thing social media has led me to? My soul purpose. No, social media itself isn't my soul purpose in life. However, it's allowed me to find a purpose that I think has meaning and might make the world a *tiny* bit better in the big picture.

When I first got into the space, social media just seemed fun and light. We were all excited about this new tech as a means of connecting with people, finding influencers to love, and getting inspired—by interior design, food, travel, photography. One thing about social media: there's a niche for everything and everyone! In the early days, the promise of the connection social media offered was so exciting.

But in the past few years, I've noticed a more negative vibe online. I'll be scrolling socials and reading comments and am often really horrified by what people say online. I have never been the victim of online abuse myself, because I'm operating behind the scenes and don't have a huge following of my own. But some of the influencers that Zink Talent represents have had really ugly experiences. The comments they get from people would make me break down and cry if I were them—luckily, most of them have developed a thick skin to it. They have to.

Not everybody escapes social media unscathed. A majority of US teenagers (59 percent) report having been bullied or harassed online.[1] One of the biggest reasons for online abuse? The way a person *looks*. Women, in particular, are vulnerable to this kind of harassment.[2] And the sad but inevitable fact is that what happens on the screen doesn't stay on the screen but has very real effects on people's mental health. I was horrified to learn that the links

---

1   Monica Anderson, "A majority of teens have experienced some form of cyberbullying," Pew Research Center, September 27, 2018, https://www.pewresearch.org/internet/2018/09/27/a-majority-of-teens-have-experienced-some-form-of-cyberbullying/.

2   Emily A. Vogels, "Teens and cyberbullying 2022," Pew Research Center, December 15, 2022, https://www.pewresearch.org/internet/2022/12/15/teens-and-cyberbullying-2022/.

between cyberbullying and suicide have become so prevalent, there is even a term for it now: cyberbullicide.[3]

I started educating myself about all of this in late 2023. At the same time, I was starting to feel sort of discontent with what I was doing in life. Like so many of the influencers I've represented, I really love working in social media—but I was starting to recognize that social media alone isn't enough to fulfill me.

It wasn't just that the work itself didn't feel purposeful. The financial rewards I was reaping from that work were losing their luster. As a poor, young twenty-something, I'd dreamed of shopping designer brands. Being able to make those purchases as Zink Talent took off was definitely a dream come true. But after a while, the adrenaline kick of a new watch or handbag wore off. I'd thought that all this "stuff" would make me a happier person. It may have given me a quick moment of gratification. But once that wore off, I was just the same person, with a lighter bank account and another glitzy possession to show for it.

This realization really hit me when I got a new Prada handbag and was so unexcited by it, I didn't even take it out of the box. It was sitting in my closet for months before I finally unpacked it. And I just felt kind of empty when I did. That's when I realized how badly I was lacking a soul purpose. Social media and its financial rewards weren't it.

Don't get me wrong, I *love* Zink Talent, and the agency has brought me so much joy. It still does. I absolutely adore what I do and the people I work with. I just also want to do something good for the world with what I've created. It's amazing that I'm able to give creators

---

3    Ariel Schonfeld, Dale McNiel, Takeo Toyoshima, and Renée Binder, "Cyberbullying and Adolescent Suicide," *The Journal of the American Academy of Psychiatry and Law* 51, no. 1 (March 2023): 112–119, https://doi.org/10.29158/JAAPL.220078-22.

opportunities and provide my team with a positive work environment (and plenty of perks)! But I'd love to make a change beyond that. Call it my final epiphany—for now, anyway!

I decided I wanted to do something. But what? As I considered the increasingly negative vibes I was seeing on socials, I identified an opportunity to leverage Zink Talent to raise awareness about online abuse—but I still had no clue exactly *what* to do.

I got back to those scrappy early days of Zink Talent and started looking up nonprofits involved in anti–online bullying initiatives. I acknowledged that I didn't have expertise in anti-bullying awareness and needed to partner with a reputable, established organization that could provide the educational resources and tangible support needed to make a difference.

I also called my publicist Mack and told her my vision (yes, instead of being the PR girl, I've now hired the PR girl—it's all come full circle)! She loved the idea and genuinely wanted to make a change, too. I only wanted to include people who believed in what I believed in, so I was so happy to hear that it resonated with her. She then set up meetings with a bunch of nonprofits in the anti-cyberbullying space.

Enter the Cybersmile Foundation, a multi-award-winning nonprofit organization committed to digital well-being. Cybersmile works to tackle all forms of bullying and abuse online, promoting kindness, diversity, and inclusion by building a safer, more positive digital community. Through education, research, awareness campaigns, and the promotion of positive digital citizenship, the organization works to reduce incidents of cyberbullying. Through professional help and support services, the organization empowers those affected and their families to regain control of their lives. Cybersmile is also responsible for launching Stop Cyberbullying Day, an international awareness day. In short, they *really* know what they're talking about.

It was the perfect fit—and the organization had already done some amazing collaborations, for example, with Rimmel London. I was excited that they even wanted to talk to me, to be honest! Then, we had our first call, and I had an amazing connection with the organization's founder. He'd been inspired to start the organization after his own daughter struggled with online hate, and his story was incredibly poignant. We clicked immediately.

By the time I got off the call, I was confident that Cybersmile was the right organization to partner with. In fact, Mack went ahead and canceled my calls with the other nonprofits I'd been considering working with. We were sure Cybersmile was it! But I admit: I still had some doubts. Not about Cybersmile or about the collaboration itself but about Zink Talent's role in the effort. I mean, I run a talent agency. Was it really my place to take a stand against cyberbullying? Could I reasonably ask the influencers I knew to participate in some initiative toward that end? Would they be willing to do it? Would anyone take me seriously? Or would they think, *Stay in your lane*?

Then, literally that same day, something happened that made me realize I *had* to speak up. It was only a few hours after that call with Cybersmile that I got a DM request from a girl I'd never met. A glance showed me that she was a mutual connection of an influencer I'd recently reconnected with—a true NYC It Girl. Gorgeous, smart, and with an eye for style, she was one of those women who was *made* for social media success.

I had met this NYC It Girl through another successful influencer who I'd idolized back in the day: @Bridget. Bridget was one of the original Insta girls I obsessed over while I was still in PR. I'd actually started working with her while I was a PR girl, and she later linked me up with this NYC It Girl. Having recently left her talent agency, the NYC It Girl was in search of new representation. Zink Talent was already well established by the time—so Bridget sent her my way. I was *so* excited that she wanted to work with me. I fangirled briefly and then, of course, signed her on. She was friendly, smart, and a dream to work with.

Then the COVID-19 pandemic hit and, like a lot of people at the time, she started to experience some mental health struggles. She was vocal about her ups and downs, which really resonated with a lot of her followers. But it was also very jarring when she first started opening up about it all—because it was so unexpected. On the surface, it seemed like she was happily married and doing well when, in fact, she was struggling. We'd all (naively) been thinking, "Wow, this girl has the perfect life, she must be so happy." Not quite. At one point she got a divorce, and then things really seemed to go downhill. She posted on social media less and less, to the point that there were Reddit threads asking what had happened to her.

But she was resilient and strong, and she picked herself up and kept on. She made it through her divorce and met someone new. She had a beautiful NYC wedding in the fall of 2023, which I went to—and it was breathtaking. I was happy for her; it seemed like she'd passed through the darkness and found the light on the other side.

It was about six months after her wedding that she told me she was planning on making a comeback to social media. We started talking about it in early 2024. She had been busy focusing on her own health and was ready to share that journey with the broader public—and we talked about ways to make that happen. Our last phone call was in March 2024, and I remember being so excited when we got off that call.

Then I got that DM from a connection of hers I didn't know personally. It turned out to be her childhood best friend. That first message read something to the effect of, *I know you were in touch recently. I have some news. Can I call you?* She'd left her number. I called her immediately. I had a weird feeling about it. You know that twisting, turning feeling you get in your stomach when you already know something is wrong? That was how I felt. Sadly, my worst fears were confirmed: that NYC It Girl I'd idolized, who had seemed to live in a perfect world, had taken her own life.

It was both saddening and baffling. I had been so sure that she'd been doing well. She had seemed optimistic and eager to make her comeback. And then, she was gone. Coming on the heels of my call with Cybersmile, that timing of the news was eerie.

And that's what pushed me to go ahead with the collaboration. While her suicide may not have been due to cyberbullying, her commitment to openly sharing her mental health journey was an inspiration. And I have no doubt she got her share of mean online comments throughout her career. By supporting this cause, I hope Zink Talent can help raise awareness—and if it helps anybody, even just one person, then that is truly a life's work I would be prouder of than any money I've made.

Now, like so many of the influencers I've worked with, I see myself finding a new soul purpose through social media. Zink Talent has officially partnered with the Cybersmile Foundation to address the issue of cyberbullying and the impact that it has on mental health through the power of creator initiatives. The partnership kicked off with an influencer-led campaign meant to inspire influencers and online communities to take a proactive stance against cyberbullying on June 21, 2024 (which was also Stop Cyberbullying Day 2024). We have more initiatives planned for the future, and I am optimistic that we can make a difference. So, in the end, social media *is* my soul purpose—it just looks a little different from what I anticipated.

# Writing My Story: Manifesting What's to Come

I've always loved bookstores. I love those picture-perfect shelves of books, the aesthetic vibe, the smell of new books—and, of course, the promise of whatever story I might discover as I browse the shelves. When I traveled to Sydney, I passed a bookstore and went in—and I pictured what it would be like to see *my* book on the shelves. Soon enough, I'll know what it feels like. I'm so proud of the story I've already completed and the many chapters I've already concluded, from the A&F era of my teen years to the PR-girl era of my twenties. Without all those other chapters behind me, even the painful ones— like the loss of my dad—my book wouldn't be complete.

At the same time, so much of my life is still unwritten. I cannot predict with absolute certainty how the social media landscape will unfold. But I trust in that innate Zink scrappiness to get me through whatever comes. Ultimately, Zink Talent is a talent agency, and there will always be talent to represent. I just manage people who are of the moment. When the industry pivots, I am ready to adapt and bring my clients with me. Because there's one thing I'm sure of: if you don't evolve in this rapidly changing industry, you *will* get kicked to the curb.

For now, I'm focusing on scaling the agency and aligning my professional path with my newfound soul purpose. And I'm still working on myself—always, always, always. I'm trying to get more in touch with my feminine energy and lead a healthier life and be more mindful. Basically, like all of us, I'm just trying to figure out this whole "adulting" thing. I'm not sure where it will all lead, but I've got some ideas, and I'm doing my best to manifest them every freaking day.

# #Inspo: Keep Writing Your Story

We all have a story to tell. If you take nothing else away from this book, I hope it's this: only *you* are in charge of your story. Take control of the narrative and make that story exactly what you want it to be. Some tips to making it your own personal bestseller:

- *Make space for your soul.* Whether it's your soulmate or your soul purpose, make space in your life for it. We all want to find a person we truly love and a purposeful path that makes us excited to grind every day, right? You know how I like to get spiritual, and I really believe the universe can only give us those things once we make space for them.

- *Listen to the epiphany.* This was something I mentioned when I first shared my "subway epiphany" about starting an influencer talent agency. Don't lose that ability to listen to the epiphanies the universe sends you. Even when your life seems "all figured out," there may be an epiphany waiting for you that could change it all.

- *Stay flexible.* Both personally and professionally, my life has taken so many unexpected turns. Being able to adapt is what's allowed me to take advantage of the various opportunities along the way. I encourage you to do the same.

Whatever you do, don't give up. If you are having a difficult time, I beg you to remember it is temporary. Everybody's book is filled with at least one tough chapter. It is only one chapter. Don't you want to see what's to come in the chapters that follow? Closing the book too soon takes away that possibility. It also means that all the people who love and admire you don't get the chance to read your book to the end. And trust me, there are people out there who want to read your book—all of it. Keep writing your story.

# Cyberbullying and Mental Health Resources

If you are struggling, there is help available. Here are some resources to keep in mind and share:

- Cybersmile has tons of educational resources, including guides to digital self-care. https://www.cybersmile.org/education

- If you are having suicidal thoughts, the National Suicide Hotline is available 24/7 to help individuals in crisis. Call 988 or visit https://suicidepreventionlifeline.org/

- Crisis Text Line is likewise available 24/7. Text "HOME" to 741741. www.crisistextline.org

There are people out there to help you. Please do not hesitate to reach out if you need support.

# CONCLUSION

# What's Next for You?

Enough about me! What about *you*?! I have no idea what your journey holds, but all I can say is please, please, please, do your best to enjoy it! Yes, I know it's easier said than done on some days. But truly, believe me, I'd say 80 percent of the things that stressed me out like crazy in my twenties were, in retrospect, not worth stressing over. That's such a cliché, but it's the truth!

Thank you for reading my book, and I hope you were able to find something useful in it (or at least get a laugh out of it). You know I'm all about manifesting, so in parting, let me manifest some things for you:

I manifest good health for you, both mental and physical.

I manifest a soulmate for you, whether that's a romantic partner, a bestie, or even your dog.

I manifest a safe and comfortable home for you, where you can feel at ease and retreat when the world gets a little bit scary.

I manifest courage for you, so you have the guts to go your own damn way and make your own path, regardless of what the rest of the world says.

I manifest a soul purpose for you, something that inspires you every day to set the world alight with your fire.

I manifest peace for you, whatever that may look like in your world.

And last but definitely not least: I manifest that you never, *ever* settle. Don't settle when it comes to a job, a city, a romantic partner—anything. You deserve better than to settle.

Stay scrappy!

XX

— Samantha

# ABOUT THE AUTHOR

Samantha Zink is the visionary talent management agency founder and CEO behind Zink Talent. Samantha has been working in the world of fashion, lifestyle, and beauty PR since 2013. Prior to Zink Talent, Samantha worked with a celebrity clientele, handled large campaigns, and collaborated with renowned brands and designers through various agencies in NYC. After witnessing the rapid rise of influencers, Samantha saw an opportunity and decided to forge her own path by venturing into managing influencers herself. Drawing from her years of experience and learning from the best in the field, Samantha launched her brand, Zink Talent, in 2018. Today, Samantha leads a dynamic team of professionals, specializing in managing collaborations and brand deals for influencers. Her impressive portfolio includes partnerships with renowned brands such as YSL Beauty, Dior Beauty, Rare Beauty, Michael Kors, Fendi, Celine, Nike, Adidas, Patrick Ta, NBA, and Charlotte Tilbury.

Printed in the USA
CPSIA information can be obtained
at www.ICGtesting.com
JSHW021906300924
70809JS00001B/1/J